The Journey

A Lifetime of
Prophetic Moments

The Journey

A Lifetime of Prophetic Moments

BY DICK IVERSON

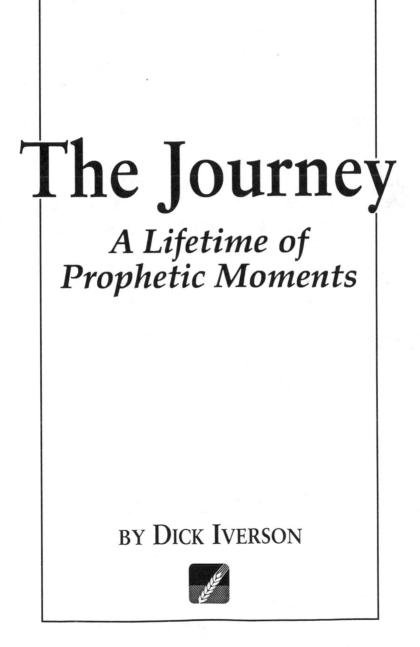

THE JOURNEY

Copyright © 1995
by Dick Iverson

Published By

BIBLE TEMPLE PUBLISHING
9200 NE Fremont
Portland, Oregon 97220
1-800-777-6057

ISBN 0-914936-02-6
Printed in the U.S.A.

ACKNOWLEDGMENTS

I wish to thank my wife, Edie, and my four daughters, Debra, Diane, Brenda and Tracey, and their husbands, Phil Zedwick, Mark Bryan, Mark Sligar and Todd Ebeling, for their constant encouragement in writing this book.

I also want to give my deep appreciation to Roxy Kidder, my personal secretary, who typed the original manuscript. Also to Larry Asplund who worked through the manuscript as well as Buck Custer who refined it. I am deeply indebted to them all.

Knowing Dick Iverson for over thirty years has been a rare privilege for me. During that time, I have seen his ministry and influence grow and expand like a fruitful bough around the world. Having ministered together in foreign countries and in churches at home, I have found him to be a man of excellent integrity and great devotion, who lives and proves the principles he advocates. I am very grateful for his personal friendship and encouragement which have been of great value to my own life and ministry.

Through the years Dick has been a diligent student of the Bible as well as God's people. This has produced rich dividends for his local church and God's work everywhere. He has excelled as a shepherd of congregations and pastors alike.

This autobiography is a book of timely importance. It is a personal account of one of God's faithful servants that will be a great inspiration to the reader. What a delight to read a success story like this and observe the faith and hope of a man and his family who have learned to trust God so fully. Great fruit has come from their combined diligence and obedience. We can all learn a tremendous amount from their living examples.

Ernest Gentile

Paul wrote to the Corinthian believers "you might have ten thousand instructors in Christ, yet you do not have many fathers" (I Cor. 4:15).

Dick Iverson has been an exemplary father in his own house and family, and he has been a father to many pastors and church leaders. I have worked closely with him for over twenty years, and I have seen a man who has a very large heart. He has room for so many that are fatherless in the kingdom of God.

Some of the qualities of Dick Iverson that stand out in my mind are these:

- A faith that believes God at all times. I have never seen him despondent even in very trying times. He is always upbeat and positive confident that God is for us and we will be victorious.

- A great love for the church, the bride of Christ. He always puts the kingdom of God and the purposes of God ahead of everything else. He believes that the church is God's instrument to extend the kingdom of God.

- A great love for the local church, Bible Temple. Even though he is in demand all over the world, he is truly in love with his home church. He constantly evaluates his personal activities as to how they affect the church.

- A personal integrity that practices what is preached. I have seen so many pastors and leaders who preach to others but who do not set the standard with their own personal life style. Dick Iverson will not ask others to do what he himself will not do.

- A true servanthood concept of leadership. Dick Iverson has demonstrated that greatness comes through dying to yourself and laying down your life for others. In his teaching and in his lifestyle he has emphasized the power of washing one another's feet.

Pastor Iverson has influenced my life like no other person. I could speak of his great wisdom, his positive leadership, his role model, his speaking abilities, but most of all I treasure him as a personal friend.

I trust this book will touch you, in at least a small way, in the same way his life has touched mine.

Bill Scheidler

PREFACE

The following is a story of our journey through life. It is not just my story or my family's story, it is a journey of a people of God, those who God individually drew to my side to fulfil His will and purpose.

Moses couldn't go into the land unless the people had the faith to do it. In Moses' day they were afraid of the walled cities and the giants, and they failed to take the land.

This is not the case with those whom the Lord identified with me. I have been overwhelmed with the quality of godly, faithful people the Lord has sent to walk with me over the years. It would have been impossible to accomplish the things the Lord allowed us to accomplish without the people of God being faithful.

It would be impossible to name all those who have stood faithfully on the wall over the last forty-four years. Many have gone on to their reward, but their names and memories I will never forget. Men and women like Warren and Pearl Steele, Chuck Bettis, Mom Swanson (Edie's mother), Ivy and Sylva Iverson (my parents), Frank and Joyce Deardorff, Mike Elrod, Morrie Iverson (my brother), LeEtta Helbling, Robin Johnson and recently, Michael Mace and Bob Estes. The list could go on and on. There are those who are still standing with me today like Alex and Esther Johansen, George and Ethel Gwinnutt, Woody and Bea Sanger, Ken and Diane Olson, Al and Phyllis Hopper, Keith and Linda Ebeling, Wayman and Sandy Steele, Alice Haines Kisaberth, Winifred Knapp, Louise Christopher, Errol and Bonnie Livesay, Bill and Barbara Roberts, Bob and Ellie Blomdahl, Larry and Lynette Andrew, John Tarter, Leota Odmark, Karen House, Ginger Iverson, my nephews and their wives, Terry and Shari Iverson and Jerry and Jean Iverson, as well as my brother Neil and his family.

Then there are the elders that have stood with me in leadership. Again, I couldn't name them all, but people like Kevin Conner, Rick and Merilee Johnston, Raul and Miriam Trujillo, David and Sue Blomgren, Ben Taylor, Mike and Marsha Herron, Ken and Connie Wilde, Frank and Sharon Damazio, Wendell and Gini Smith, Bill and JoAnne Scheidler, Ken and Glenda Malmin, Jack and Libby Louman, Howdy and Georgia Sligar, Ed and Dorcas Mason, Bob and Sue MacGregor, Larry and Karen Knox, Art and Randi Johansen, Larry and Lynda Asplund, Lanny and Joanne Hubbard, Steve and Debbie Trujillo, Bob and Jane Isabell, Jan and Sylvia Weinstein, Joel and Robbin Hjertstedt, Barry and Charmayne Brandt, Howard and Donna Rachinski, Ernie and Ida Rachinski, Leif and Leona Malmin, Steve and Julia Allen, Larry and Carolyn Wade and Bob and Sharon Wagar. If your name is not mentioned, please know it is only because I don't have the room to mention all of the approximately fifty elders that have served with me and are serving with me to this day.

I also want to say with the Apostle Paul that God has placed by my side godly women. Starting with my wife, Edie, who has been my best supporter, as well as my four daughters, Debra, Diane, Brenda and Tracey. Others, like Marcia Duffel, Barbara Wright, Roxy Kidder, Joanne Noble, Merrilee Mobley, Cheryl Bolton and Janice Dorszynski. Again, the list could go on and on.

I wish to also include my four sons-in-law, Phil Zedwick, Mark Bryan, Mark Sligar and Todd Ebeling for their loyalty and encouragement and for standing with me.

This is the story of a journey of a people of God under my leadership.

DICK IVERSON

L ife is not just a series of minutes, hours, days and years flowing out before us in a straight line. Life is a series of interconnected prophetic moments - set times, mountain peaks along the journey - that form us and make us who we are. That has certainly been true in my life.

⭐⭐

I came into this world in a very humble fashion. I was born in Sherburn, Minnesota, a town of about a thousand people in the southern part of the State. The year was 1930. I was the third of three sons born to Lawrence "Ivy" and Sylvia Iverson. My oldest brother was Morrie and my second brother Neil, and there were only three years and three months between Morrie's birth and my own. Our friends used to call the Iverson brothers "Tom, Dick, and Harry": Morrie's middle name was Thomas, I was Dick and Neil was Harry.

The first significant moment in my life came

very early. My beginning was very precarious
according to my parents. I was born with a double
hernia, and in those days they could do nothing for
me. I was unable to hold down any food, and I was
dying. Six weeks after my birth I weighed less than
when I was born.

Out of desperation, my parents took their dying
baby to their little Assembly of God church to ask
for prayer. They laid me on the altar and asked
the pastor, Willard Pope, if he would anoint my
body with oil and pray the prayer of faith--which of
course he did.

They didn't know it immediately, but that night
a miracle took place. Mom and Dad took me
home, and for the first time in six weeks I was able
to take in food and hold it down. I began to grow
and thrive, and I have been thriving every since.

My parents were pillars in the Sherburn
Assembly. I clearly remember that every time the
doors of the church were open for a service, the
Iverson family was there. My dad was a strong
leader, but it was my mom who was the creative
one. She was very involved in drama, and I
remember her once playing in a production called
"The Missing Christian." Mom was the preacher of
our family which explains why I've always been a
supporter of women preachers.

The next key moment in my life took place in
Minnesota too. When I was eight years old I
remember sitting in a tent meeting listening to an
evangelist preach about the fact that all sinners are
going to hell, but that those who turn to the Lord
in faith will be saved. I remember taking it

personally, applying it to my own life. And all of a sudden I knew that *I* was going to hell.

I remember to this day the conviction of the Holy Spirit that came over me. I felt like something akin to Al Capone, though of course at that point I had no idea that there was an Al Capone. I experienced tremendous conviction of sin and knew my stealing cookies and telling lies had caught up with me. It wasn't a laughing matter; I was absolutely serious! I knew that if I died that moment I would go to hell.

I remember walking down a literal saw dust trail to the altar, and there, as a wretched sinner of eight, weeping over my sins and asking Jesus to come into my life. And He did! And he's remained faithfully in my life ever since.

Mom had serious respiratory problems and every winter we would escape the Minnesota ice and snow by coming out west. In 1938, our pastor moved to Portland, Oregon, so my parents decided to move West permanently as well. We were going to settle either in Los Angeles or Portland where Brother Pope was.

> The Lord directs our steps in many and varied ways.

My dad was leaning toward going to California where the weather would be better for Mom, but when we arrived at Salt Lake City we were caught in a big snow storm and the highway to Los Angeles was closed. So we settled in Portland.

Was that snow storm that set the course of the rest of my life just coincidence? I don't think so. The Lord directs our steps in many and varied ways. He brought that snow storm in front of our path in 1938, and I've been in Portland, Oregon ever since.

In Portland we went to several churches. At first we attended Willard Pope's Calvary Tabernacle. I don't know what happened but that church soon dissolved and we began attending a Foursquare church in the Parkrose district of Portland where I was wonderfully baptized in the Holy Spirit. I was

Life is a series of interconnected prophetic moments

overwhelmed by the Spirit in a powerful way, finding myself stretched out on the floor and speaking in tongues for over an hour. This experience was another prophetic moment in my life. I was eleven years old at the time and the Lord revealed Himself to me in a personal and meaningful way. The Lord didn't come to me in a blaze of fire but spoke to me so clearly that, from that age on, I knew God had called me into the ministry. I didn't know entirely what that meant, but I did know I was going to be a preacher.

In 1943, we began to attend a church close to our home - in the very area where I now pastor. A new Pentecostal Church of God called Montavilla Tabernacle had just been planted, and the Iversons became one of the first families in the church. I was thirteen years old at the time, and I was baptized in water there.

I remember hating to go to that church which was very rowdy Pentecostal. We met in an old quonset type building that was always dirty and smelly. It was in the neighborhood where I lived, and my paper route went right by the church building. I remember sneaking into services and hoping none of my friends would see me.

So my teenage years were not always happy. My father was very harsh and restrictive, a short Norwegian who believed children were "to be seen but not heard". He most upset me by not allowing me to participate in sports. I wanted above all to be a professional baseball player, and there was no way he would allow that. Every day after school I came home to a long list of chores. I did them as quickly as possible so I could play ball on the field across the street. But I could only play until I heard his Model A Ford coming down the street about 5:15. Then very soon he would call my name, and I knew that was the end of my fun. In fact, I never felt as if he loved me. He often called me "Sloppy Jack" after an uncle who had particuarly disgusting manners; and so (perhaps as a result) I always had a loose button or an unfastened belt. Also, it seemed he would always give the best of things to my two older brothers - whether it was clothes or toys or whatever. While I could never figure it out completely, still I noticed it and it always hurt.

During my sophomore year in high school I was doing very well, academically and socially, but because it was a co-educational high school my dad soon transferred me to an all-boys technical high school. At this time, the only thing that was important to our family was going to church. Not only was sports a low priority so was education. Quite often we went to church every night of the week. If we had homework we just had to leave it undone so we could go to the meeting. My dad had succeeded in business without an education, so he just didn't see the point.

When I was about 15 years old my dad and I were having an argument, which was the first of only two times in my life that I've ever been out of control angry. Dad had told me "No" one too many times, and I bristled, rose up and said, "I've had it with you, Dad! I'm through!

> *The fear of the Lord . . . can keep us in a moment of crisis.*

I'm leaving and I'm not coming back!" I walked through the front door and slammed it, something we never did, then I marched out to the street and was dead serious determined to hitchhike to Los Angeles. 'I was never coming back. My dad was never going to boss me around again!'

Then I heard a voice behind me: "Young man! You get back in here, and you get back in here now!" and because I had the fear of Dad in me, I froze when I heard his voice. If I hadn't, there's no telling where I would be today.

The fear of the Lord works in much the same way. It can keep us in a moment of crisis, when we're tempted to do something foolish. If we have been trained up in the Lord, we will tend to obey Him when we're in deep waters.

This was not only a "set time," it was one of *the* crossroads of my life. Fear of my dad kept me. I stopped and returned to the house. I don't remember anything else of the rest of that day. But it saved my life. Also, it was one of the events that caused me to think a lot about fatherhood over the years. I believe that a father's role is even *more* important than is generally understood and goes beyond the merely visible headship of his family, because in fact, a childs' first concept of God comes from their natural father. If a father is overly harsh and restrictive, the grown children naturally will think of God as harsh and out to get them. This does not imply that there is no place for discipline because understanding the concept of "disobedience equals pain" is *absolutely* essential in developing a healthy fear of the Lord. However, restriction must be balanced always with equal parts love. If a child gets spanked, he should always get a hug afterward as well. In my lifetime, too, I have seen a number of spiritual

> *Restriction must be balanced always with equal parts love.*

leaders fail morally - and inevitably it's happened when they have lost the fear of God - ie., forgotten this disobedience/pain principle. Is it any wonder that the enemy is fighting so hard to do away with spanking, cloaking his evil designs under the general, catch all banner of "child abuse"? The disobedience/pain concept - passed down to us and ingrained in us by our earthly fathers - becomes our absolute anchor in times of tempting and testing. It becomes a chief protector, keeping us on a safe and Godly journey. Ultimately if we believe that God can't lie, then we must know from His Word that, if we sin, He will always deal with us, no matter who we are. This is an immutable law: we do reap what we sow, and the discipline/pain principle is the controller over what we sow.

One of the highest mountain peaks on my journey occurred at age seventeen. One night I went with my pastor to the Pentecostal Church of God in Clackamas, Oregon, for a fellowship night. I took my bass viol and he took his accordion; we sang and played and he preached. While we were ministering, I noticed a beautiful blonde in the congregation. She was from the Oregon City Foursquare Church, visiting the Clackamas church for the first time; and, though I tried to meet her, she wouldn't give me the time of day. I found out later she thought I was too old for her, even though I was only one year older. Still, I was at least able to get her name - Edie Swanson.

I thought of her often afterwards and decided to pursue her. About a month later, in October, I attended a party sponsored by our two youth groups, and I spent that entire evening trying to get to know her. When we played "bobbing for apples" I saw where she was in line and made sure I was in the same place in the other line so we would end up together. I did the same thing in several other games that we played and as the evening wore on, the wall came down. Edie began to talk to me - obviously aware of my efforts to get acquainted. I continued to flirt with her, and she made no effort to discourage me, not choosing to sit and talk with many of the other young men, including the one who had accompanied her to the party.

I was elated at this successful first in our lives and offered her, her brother and a neighbor boy a ride home. She, her brother, and friend sat in the back seat and I sat in the front passenger seat, turning around to talk with Edie all the way to her house, while another young church brother did the driving. Her friend, sat in silence, having endured a whole evening of my intrusion. In a way, that helped to make the experience unforgettable - as were many of our other early encounters.

I continued to court Edie in the following weeks. As a matter of fact, I almost lost my job at the church as a result. I was paid $5 a week to clean the church building and while I was there I called Edie - long distance to Oregon City. Of course when the pastor found out he confronted me about it and told my parents, so that the phone calls, if not the romance, ceased. Later, after seeing each other at three or four more church related group gatherings, there came the time for our first real date. My parents were away but, surprisingly, my dad had given me permission to use his Model A Ford to take Edie to another youth fellowship meeting and out to dinner afterwards.

Well, the meeting got out rather late. Then it seemed we became absolutely mesmerized with each other in the restaurant where we talked and talked until about 1:00 a.m. I wasn't worried about my parents since they were away, but as it turned out, I should have been very worried about Mom Swanson, Edie's mom, whom I still scarcely knew. She was a Swedish single parent who raised Edie and her brother with great strictness and, when Edie didn't arrive home as expected, she became frantic, telephoning the police and hospitals to find out if there had been an accident. She was sitting by the door with her head on the table when we came in and she proceeded to jump up and read me the riot act in her thick accent. "Vats da matta vith you?" she shouted at me. "Vat kind of man are you?" I stood with one hand on the door knob and a voice inside telling me to "run, run!" I was genuinely afraid and had no answer for her, having been thoroughly schooled in not talking back to adults. I stayed, enduring the tirade which went on for a seemingly interminable time, but which I admittedly deserved. Then finally, after the first wave had passed, Edie intervened and brought calm. She told her mother everything we had done that evening being sure to say "everything's all right."

I have often thought, too, that if I had obeyed that voice of fear in me - the one that said "run, run!" - my whole life would have been different, and not near as fulfilled. I wasn't in love with Edie yet and, had I run, I would have been too embarrassed to ever go back. Thank the good Lord I stayed!

Afterwards, I got back in the Model A Ford and decided to set a land speed record going home. There was no reason to - my parents weren't home - but I did it anyway, making the normal thirty minute trip from Oregon City in exactly fifteen. Then I ran in the house and wrote Edie a letter, apologizing to her and her mother for keeping her out so late. At the bottom of the letter I put a P.S.

bragging that I had made it home in fifteen minutes. Unfortunately though, I left the letter out on the table and in the morning when my parents came home they found it. More unfortunately, they also read it - which was simply "the end of the world."

Not only was I told in clear, ringing terms that I would never touch the car again, but now my parents had a poor opinion of Edie as well. 'What kind of worldly girl would be keeping their sweet innocent son out until that hour?' In fact, it took a *very* long time afterwards for them to recognize Edie as the good girl she always was.

Of course everything was slower back then. For instance, it took a whole year of "going together" before I was able to kiss Edie for the first time; and that was an unforgettable circumstance in more than the obvious way.

I was over visiting Edie in her house on a cold winter's day. Mom Swanson was gone to the grocery store, and Edie and I were standing with our backs to the fireplace trying to get warm. The fire was crackling; it was sort of dark, I remember, and the atmosphere was just right. For quite awhile I had been thinking that at some point in time I needed to kiss this girl. Trouble was, I really didn't know how to do it coming from such a restrictive background. All I knew for certain was that it was not supposed to be like kissing your mother - that it needed to be longer and more passionate. I leaned towards her and she must have known it was coming because she didn't draw back. Then as I held her with my lips pressed to hers - and it was so good to finally hold her! - I determined I would prolong it and let her know just what kind of a man was holding her. I held her even tighter and that was about the time that Edie began to squirm and struggle strangely - causing me to have the fleeting thought that I might have some strange power over women - until she broke free, exclaiming "Ouch, the fire's burning my legs!" Forever afterwards, we would remember that first kiss as our "kiss of fire."

One of the key events of my life occurred during the summer of 1947 at the William Branham meetings in Portland. He spent at least a week in Portland; I attended every meeting, and afterwards I was never the same. The Lord began to stir in my heart specifically about ministry during that time.

I remember seeing a deaf and dumb child healed in the services. When he was healed everyone heard him say, "Mama...Papa." And when the piano played in the background he whirled around, looking for the sound. I remember seeing a demon possessed man march onto the platform and threaten Brother Branham, only to be pushed low by the power of God.

I graduated from high school early, in January of 1948. I was still only seventeen years old and that turned out to be one of the most important years of my life.

At that time, my family was becoming increasingly involved in ministry. We would travel to little churches and minister. Dad played the accordion, Mom the piano, and I played the bass and sang. Mom had been healed of her respiratory problems and would share her dynamic message of faith.

Then something very sad and disillusioning happened. One of the youth leaders in our district, a leader I greatly idolized, my spiritual hero, was found to be living in adultery along with a number of other preachers in our district. These were all people I looked up to. They were my leaders, the ones I had been following, and now they had fallen to the ground. Suddenly my world came crumbling down as well.

I was seventeen years of age, wanting to go into the ministry, but totally losing confidence in the organization with which I was involved. I found myself in a no man's land, in a dry and barren wilderness, and I didn't know what to do. I didn't know how I was ever going to go into the ministry, yet there was a deep love for God remaining in my heart.

Given this discouragement with my spiritual leaders, I just wanted to leave town and start a new life on my own. By this time, I had come to hate my dad. He had always told me that when I turned eighteen I was free to leave the house and do whatever I wanted to but until then I had to do what he told me to do. So I was just waiting to turn eighteen - which I wouldn't do until July following my graduation from high school.

I remember about that time my parents wanted me to go with them to Orofino, Idaho for ministry. I didn't want to go but, my dad used the fact that I wasn't yet eighteen as a means for forcing me.

When July and my birthday came, I told Dad that I was leaving. I remember his being angry because he wanted me to keep on traveling with him - to continue being a part of his ministry team, playing the bass. I began to take some shirts from the closet and Dad said, "Take 'em all. Because when you leave, you're not coming back!" I remember throwing my clothes into the suitcase and hearing my mom crying in the background. Needless to say, I didn't leave on the best of terms.

My dad had run away from home at the age of thirteen after the death of his mother and had only completed the eighth grade. Looking back, I must say Dad was doing his best raising us boys but, unfortunately, I didn't see that then. He and I were always clashing, in fact, I had become so bitter I wished he were dead.

After leaving, I joined a friend of mine who was working in Richland, Washington at the Hanford atomic energy plant. At first I worked two jobs in Richland, at the atomic energy plant during the day and at a drug store in the evening. But surprisingly, things changed for the better. A Christian man whom I had met there resigned from his job as foreman in one of the major construction warehouses and, on leaving, recommended me for the job. In doing so, he mentioned that I had just "graduated from school" - which I found out later was interpreted to mean I had just finished college rather than just high school.

To make a long story short, I got the job which was high paying and about which I knew virtually

nothing. There was, though, an older man there -
a veteran in the place, who knew most everything
about everything and legitimately should have
been given the job. I approached him with hat in
hand and told him I knew nothing and that he
could just tell me what to do. He agreed most
graciously saying that he would help me. He did
so too, to the extent that I soon won rave reviews
for the "job I was doing." (I've often thought since
then that this was my introduction to team
ministry).

Living in the government barracks then and
eating the cafeteria food that was provided, I was
able to save nearly all of my money and in just
five weeks bought a new suit of clothes and my
own car. I bought a jet black '41 Chevy with
"Hollywood hubcaps" and a grey plaid suit with a
bright red tie. Boy did I think I was hot!

I remember driving home in my new car and
new suit. I had told Mom I was coming but hadn't
told my dad wanting to surprise him and show
him that I didn't need him. So, I came swaggering
in as if I had conquered the world.

I wasn't disappointed by his reaction either. At
first his eyes grew real wide, as he saw I was driving
a car newer and better than his; then afterward he
was real silent while I visited with my mom.

She, of course, oohed and ah-ed over the car
and my clothes and said I had done "real well."
After a short time of visiting I stood up and said I
was going to see Edie. While my mother pleaded
with me not to leave so soon, Dad continued his
silence, unable to boss me and confronted with the

fact - that now I was a grown man with my own money and car.

In retrospect, I believe the whole experience was divinely appointed, not designed to put my dad down, but essentially to build in me the self-respect my father had failed to impart. I believe God said, "I'll help the kid out", and in letting me succeed in the warehouse foreman job He had created for me, He began to rid me of the inferiority complex which my father had fueled in various ways. It says in His holy Word that if father and mother forsake you, He will not; and if friends and church family fail you, He won't fail you. I came to understand that life doesn't end because you have a few bumps in childhood. He will take you and help you through life and give you a future. He is all you have to hold onto in the night, but if you let go of Him, then you're really in trouble.

> *Life doesn't end because you have a few bumps in childhood.*

I think that in restructuring me with new self esteem, the Lord helped me to understand my father leading ultimately to healing and reconciliation. This in turn allowed me to be a better father to my children. In fact, it allowed me to escape the passing on of bitterness to my children by doing the same things to them that had been done to me.

It wasn't until later, after I had gotten married and was the co-pastor of the church with Dad at the age of twenty-two that the Lord really began to deal with me about that bitterness. The Lord spoke to me once and said, "Your dad has taught you a lot." And I knew he had taught me a lot, but I thought only by negative example.

Eventually I was genuinely convicted by the Lord and went to my dad. "I want to thank you" I said "for everything you've taught me." He looked at me and began to weep.

At first I thought he believed I was criticizing him for teaching negatively and that he was hurt by it. But then he said, "Son, I've waited for years for you to thank me for *something*." Which is when I finally acknowledged just how much he had given himself for me down through those years. He had fed me, clothed me, taken care of me for eighteen years after all; and now I was married, in the ministry, doing well.

We embraced each other and wept in each others arms, and we were fully reconciled. The bondage of my bitterness was broken in that moment of time. And to my dad's dying day we were great friends. Bitterness would have destroyed my life and my ministry. Choosing not to deal with bitterness is *always* a fatal mistake.

T he whole time at Hanford I was in a spiritual vacuum with no sense of direction, but God was still with me and helped me through those troublesome times. In fact, He spared my life there on at least three separate occasions.

❧

When I first began, I was on the midnight shift operating an "oiler"- a large oil truck. My job was to service the big "cat" bulldozers that were a part of the project. I worked with some pretty tough guys who quickly concluded I was a Christian because I didn't smoke. They mocked me mercilessly and called me "preacher."

One night a novice driver was moving a "cat" back to the oiler truck where I was working. I was standing with my back against the bed of the truck with the blade of the cat heading in my direction. Just as the driver was about to stop the cat he missed the handle, and instead of stopping, the bulldozer lurched forward. As it did, one of my co-workers dove at me and knocked me out of the way. When we got up from the ground, we noticed that the blade had stopped an inch and a half from the bed of the truck where I was standing.

The whole event so shook up my rescuer that he later confessed to me that he was a backslidden Christian. He told me how he had secretly admired me for my Christian stand and wanted to come back to the Lord.

> *The Lord can use us to bear good fruit even during the dry seasons of our lives.*

I was able to pray with him that night, and he quickly became my best friend, an amazing illustration of how the Lord can use us to bear good fruit even during the dry seasons of our lives.

The person who was my anchor during that time was Edie. She was a very strong Christian who believed in me and kept me on track, and my love for her gave me a reason to live. Edie was so faithful, speaking only positive words and encouraging me through the hard times with my dad.

My parents left Portland to travel with our pastor, who had become a very successful evangelist, as his business managers. However, I was able to come home some weekends to see Edie and go to church with her. Apart from that, I never attended church during that dry season in my life. I thought I was too busy for church. Fortunately, I was also too busy to get into trouble.

One weekend I was traveling home to see Edie,

UPPER LEFT: Age 6. ABOVE: My brother Neil and me. LEFT: Age 18. BELOW: My family in 1945.

UPPER LEFT:
First evangelistic
meeting, Dec
1949 - Jamaica.
LEFT: Jamaica.
BELOW: The
tent I helped put
up and take down
for a well-known
evangelist.

RIGHT: Engagement photo, 1949.

LEFT: 1951. **BOTTOM:** Our wedding - 1950.

UPPER LEFT: Our first home for one year - 21' Trailer.
LEFT: Ireland.
BELOW: Ireland.

RIGHT: 1955 with
our daughter Debra.

LEFT: Edie leading worship in Ireland. **BELOW:** Newspaper clipping.

Bible Deliverance
Campaign continues in Armagh

Blind See ! Deaf Hear ! Lame Walk ! and all manner of Sickness and Diseases Healed !

EVANG K. R. IVERSON, U.S.A.

and **MR. W. DAVIDSON, Song Leader**

AT THE

City Cinema, 8.15 p.m., Sunday, August 1st

Continuing in the

City Hall, 8.15 p.m., Mon., Tues., Wed.

(LARGE HALL)

— EVERYONE WELCOME —

These signs shall follow them that Believe. M K 16, v. 17

ABOVE: Our first photo Christmas card - 1952. LEFT: My parents - 1962.

RIGHT: Edie and I in 1959.

LEFT: 1956 - My dad and me on our way to Cuba. **BELOW:** SE 80th and Washington - Montavilla Tabernacle 1955.

BELOW: My brothers Morrie & Neal with Edie and me, our daughter Debra and Morrie's wife Ginger and children.

going too fast on what is now the "Scenic Highway" through the Columbia River Gorge. I had made the trip from Richland, Washington to Portland, Oregon so many times that I was able to do it from 10:00 p.m. to 3:00 a.m., nonstop - too fast around the curves in that '41 Chevy.

When going around one curve I saw a car weaving from side to side, coming in my direction. Just before it got to me, it swerved into my lane, heading straight for me. My only choices were to hit the car head on, go over the side of the cliff, or go into the ditch and bounce off the side of the mountain on the left hand side. At the last second I turned into the ditch. I remember bouncing and bouncing, sure that I would flip the car over, but before I knew it the car had righted itself and was headed back to Portland down the right way in the right lane.

I immediately thought of what a masterful piece of driving I had just achieved. I only wished someone had been in the car to witness it. Then I heard the Lord say to me, "Next time you're on your own, Son!" I was so shaken I pulled the car over and repented as quickly as I could, thanking the Lord for his miraculous preservation.

Months went by and I began to wonder what would become of my life. I didn't know how to prepare for ministry. I had no contact with a Bible college and I had lost all confidence in the denomination in which I had grown up in. In fact, during the winter of 1948-49 almost everyone was convinced Jesus was coming back at any minute, and very few even considered formal preparation

for ministry. The atomic bomb had been dropped;
Israel had become a nation, and the return of the
Lord was surely imminent.

In June of 1949 Edie graduated from high school
and we became engaged to be married. In fact, I
gave her an engagement ring as her graduation
present. Her mother wanted her to go to Oregon
State to get her degree, but I proposed to her by
saying, "I don't want my wife to go to Oregon
State." Before we could be married, we both
realized that my dilemma of how to prepare for
ministry had to be resolved.

After a full year of working in Washington, I
received a letter from my former pastor asking if I
would be interested in joining his evangelistic
party on the road. He was doing a great work for
the Lord in that day; God had blessed him
mightily and his meetings were attracting as many
as 8,000 people a night. He wanted me to be his
"tent boy", and he actually asked if my brother
Neil and I both would come, though he would only
pay a single wage between us.

Immediately my heart leapt! Perhaps this
would be an opportunity for me to get into the
ministry. I could begin by driving the vehicles,
sleeping in the tent, and helping out in general as
we moved from city to city, thinking that maybe in
the afternoon meetings I would be allowed to lead
the song service or at least do something that
would begin to develop the call I felt in my heart.

I still suffered under an inferiority complex
stemming partly from the fact that we had moved
and changed schools several times, I had gaps in

my education and, also, no confidence in my ability to speak publicly or lead. On top of that, my view of God, at least part of the time, was that He was a tyrant looking for a chance to beat me down.

My parents encouraged me to join the evangelistic party. They said Neil and I could eat our meals with them so I would be able to save most of the half wage I would earn. This was important because I was planning to marry Edie within a year.

I did travel back to Redding, Pennsylvania, where a large healing crusade was in progress. At the same time Edie traveled to the Sharon Bible Institute in North Battleford, Saskatchewan, Canada, where a tremendous revival was underway. In fact, that revival (and Edie's experiences there) would have long range implications for Bible Temple and our ministry. The "latter rain" outpouring, as it was called, became a major stream of the Holy Spirit emphasizing praise and worship (with its power to open the Word), along with prophecy and the laying on of hands. It was within that movement that the roots of the charismatic movement originated.

At the same time, it was quite an experience for me just to walk into the huge, filled to capacity tent in Redding. I saw my former pastor, only six years older than I, now a famous healing evangelist, preaching and praying for the sick. Hundreds of people were coming to Christ and miracles were taking place every night. I was

overwhelmed!   I saw the power of God
demonstrated as I had only seen it once before, two
years earlier at the William Branham meetings, and
it really stirred me! I realized again that God was
real and that His power was available to those who
believed.

One of my assignments at the meetings was to
help people up to the platform to be prayed for
and then to escort them back down. In this way, I
personally witnessed countless miracles. I was also
responsible for being an usher, straightening things
up after the meeting, and just being available
during the day for whatever tasks might arise.
Still, I was hoping I would have a chance to have
some experience in public ministry, but that didn't
seem to be working out.

I believe that sometimes when God is dealing
with one of His servants He allows those over him
to do or say things they normally wouldn't, just so
a valuable lesson can be learned. I believe that's
what happened to me. God was going to test me
through my former pastor before He opened the
doors of ministry to me.

Jesus was tested after He had fasted forty days -
tempted to turn the stones into bread. He was
tempted to use his gift to feed himself and this is a
test I believe all ministries have to pass. Are you in
it for yourself - for the money, for your own
personal blessing - or are you in it to bless others?

I remember that night after night there was a
tremendous amount of money being given and one
of my tasks was to help count the money. As I
counted it in a room with several others, the table

would literally be piled high with money, yet, at the same time, Neil and I never received the weekly wage we had been promised.

After a few weeks, we moved the tent from Redding, Pennsylvania, to Athens, Tennessee. Then the evangelist gave us each $35. We had been with him for a number of weeks by then and this was the first money that was given to us. Still I was intimidated by this man of God. If he could work such miracles there was no telling what he might be able to do. Thus I didn't have the nerve to ask him where the rest of the money was though my view was that he had promised us a certain amount and had not kept his promise.

I went to my father and asked him if he would talk to the evangelist, but his report back was that the evangelist claimed he had intended to pay us only when we moved the tent. That meant we would each get $35 about once every month. Needless to say, that was not what I had understood. Thirty-five dollars a month was not enough money to save for my marriage the following summer. Once again, I was very disillusioned with my spiritual leader.

I was tempted night after night. As I counted the offerings I looked at the pile of money and thought how easy it would be just to slip a little into my pocket. It really was mine, after all. He had promised it to me. He was not keeping his word and so it really wouldn't be stealing. There were many nights when I was all alone with the money, holding a $20 bill in my hand and thinking about it seriously. I thank God to this day that I did not steal any of that money when I had the opportunity.

Time went on, and I realized that with such a small income I wouldn't be able to keep on much longer. In addition, I wasn't getting any public ministry experience. I wasn't being trained for the ministry and I was running out of reasons for staying with the program. Just taking care of the tent and traveling from town to town was not enough, and I was becoming very discouraged, to say the least.

At that time, my father came to Neil and me and said that he had talked to the evangelist again about our finances. He said the evangelist realized we were disappointed and were not getting what we had hoped for but he said that, if we would stay with him, he would take us with him to the mission field and pay our way. His schedule was going to take him to Jamaica, Cuba and other islands in the West Indies that very winter.

Since in those days to go overseas was a wonderful experience, I thought it would be worth all the sacrifice. In fact, I was very excited about this new opportunity and so continued to work for a few dollars and another promise.

We were in Corpus Christi, Texas by now. It was nearly December and not too far away from the time when we would be traveling overseas for the winter months. At this time another low point of my life came upon me. Again, it was God who was allowing a man of God to treat me in such a way as to prove whether or not my motive for ministry was pure. Just as He tested and proved and humbled His people in the wilderness, so He was humbling and proving me.

My father came to me that night in Corpus Christi and said the evangelist had just asked him to tell Neil and me that there was not enough money to take us to the mission field. We would have to stay in Miami, get a job, and wait until he and my parents returned to the States. I was devastated!

How many times could I put up with my leaders, supposedly spiritual men of God, lying to me and living a lie? I was completely disillusioned - with spiritual leaders, with the ministry, with the church! My last hero had fallen! My eyes had been on this man of God as they had formerly been on the fallen young youth leader, and I just couldn't believe that a man of God, a man for whom God opened blind eyes and unstopped deaf ears would lie to me again. It was the last straw!

Now what was I going to do? I had come from a very strict background where it seemed like if anything was fun it was a sin. As I have said, my dad would never let me go out for sports because they were too worldly, and one of the worst things we as Christians could ever do was go to movies. If you went to a movie and Jesus returned while you were in the movie house, you would go to hell. In fact, when you walked into that theater, that den of iniquity, the Holy Spirit left you and you were immediately in a backslidden condition. At least that's what I had been taught.

That night it was my turn to sleep in the tent. I had just counted the offering and seen more piles of money on the tables. Then we had received the news that we were not going to be able to go to the mission field because of a lack of money. I was overwhelmed with discouragement and just wanting to quit. I remember driving from my father's trailer house to the tent around 11:00, actually weeping with disappointment and disillusionment. This is when I made the decision that I was going to backslide. I would just turn my life over to the devil, I thought, which in immediate terms simply meant I'd go to a movie.

I drove around Corpus Christi trying to find a theater. I decided if I was going to backslide I might as well do a good job of it and find a really dirty movie, a "girlie" movie. I remember going into the "sleazy" part of town to find such a cheap movie house where I could go in and backslide. To that point it was the lowest night of my life.

I finally found a theater, and, never having been in a theater before, I didn't even know how to buy a ticket. I went up to the ticket window with my collar turned up so no one would see me and felt all eyes were upon me, recognizing me as a member of the evangelistic party. I purchased the ticket, knowing that I was about to leave the presence of the Lord and backslide, about to go into the lobby where the Holy Spirit would lift from me, and from where - should Jesus come - I would go to burn in hell forever.

When I walked into the lobby, I didn't know I was supposed to give half of the ticket to the man at the door. I just walked past him and hurried into the theater. Suddenly I heard a loud voice saying, "Hey you, come back here!" and thought it was God!

I shook with fear and turned around, to see the man scowling at me and asking for my ticket. I fumbled for it, then gave it to him, walked into that den of iniquity, and sat in the back row.

To this day, I don't remember what happened on the screen. I just sat in the back row and wept through the whole movie, knowing that my life was in ruins. I had backslidden, rejected the Lord and I was alone. The Holy Spirit had left me, and my life was over.

I returned to the tent at 1:00 or 2:00 in the morning, to sleep the rest of the damp, cold night, depressed and spent.

When I awoke the next morning though, I was better able to analyze my situation. I still didn't know whether or not I was called to preach, but I did have a few hundred dollars in the bank and thought if I paid my own way to Jamaica, maybe someone there would give me the opportunity to try. I had to know. I thought, "If I'm not called, I still will be returning to Portland to marry Edie Swanson and we will still be good church members. So what do I have to lose?"

I told my dad I wanted to go to Jamaica and that I would pay my own fare. Also, I distinctly remember telling my parents, "When I go to Jamaica, please don't tell anyone that I can't preach." I thought people there would see I was a part of the evangelistic party and wouldn't know I had never preached before. I was hoping that perhaps I could ask to go out to some church and preach, and would find out once and for all if the ministry was my calling.

The very first day in Jamaica we found ourselves sitting on a veranda with the island's bishop of the Church of God (of Cleveland, Tennessee). He was the overseer of approximately two hundred churches which were sponsoring the evening crusade in Kingston. Being there with him at that moment, I had the immediate feeling that my opportunity had come. Before I could say anything though, I heard my mother say, "Our son, Dick, would like to start preaching. Do you have a church where he can go and learn how to preach?" I couldn't believe it! I had specifically told my mother not to tell anyone I couldn't preach so I could have an opportunity to try. Now she was saying that although I had never preached before, I would like to get started and needed a place to practice.

You can't imagine how upset I was! It seemed as though I was trapped on a roller coaster of disappointment and discouragement. Everything was going wrong. I had paid my own way over to give this thing of ministry one last chance, and now I was sure the bishop would never open any door for me. Sure enough, the ensuing week went by and nothing happened for me. Oh sure, the island was beautiful and exotic and different, and the crusade in Kingston was going great with many marvelous miracles taking place. However I couldn't get away from the discouraging thought that my last opportunity was slipping by me. No one would give me a chance now. No one!

One day though, while I was sitting in the home where I was staying, the phone rang. It was a call from the Barberton Baptist Church. Their pastor had broken his leg and had called the bishop sponsoring the healing crusade to see if there was anybody who could preach in his church the following Sunday. I heard my Dad say, "Dick, would you like to go down and preach at a Baptist church?" which was music to my ears. My immediate answer was, "Absolutely!"

I went down to the church on Saturday to post a cardboard sign I had made:

HEALING - REVIVAL!
Every Night
Special Singing
Conducted by the Iversons
From the U.S.A.
Tell Everyone!

My time had come! Still, I had received the message loud and clear - that the Lord opens doors in His own time and not necessarily when I thought He would or should.

CHAPTER 3

Often times on our journey, prophetic moments - God's set times - come into our lives as a unique window of opportunity. The Lord provides these key moments but we must respond. We need eyes to see the significance of the moment. We need faith to reach out and seize the moment before it passes us by. It is possible to miss our "day of visitation."

☜☞

For me the moment of truth had now come. Was I called to the ministry or not? Suddenly I realized I was going to be the preacher in a meeting that would depend upon what I had to say. Would God be with me or not?

I remember fasting for three days to make sure there was nothing between the Lord and me that would hinder His responding to me. I sought the Lord diligently and studied hard. With my limited experience in the Word of God, I gathered together all of the scriptures I could find on the subject of divine healing.

On the first night of the meetings, I remember my brother and I riding our bicycles to the Barbican Baptist Church. Yes, I was scared, and yes I was feeling inadequate to the task. But I needed to find out, whether or not the Lord was calling me into the ministry, once and for all.

The church was a small and rundown, unpainted wooden structure which would have been considered the poorest of churches in America, but which was about the norm for Jamaica. Inside there were benches spaced on the rough board floor, and the altar consisted of a wood table raised one step above the main level. The church would seat a maximum of fifty and was lighted for evening services by two or three kerosene lanterns. When I arrived there were only a dozen or so people there, but, I was glad for anybody who would listen to me and give me a chance. Without the pastor there, the entire service was in my hands. After singing a couple of hymns, I began to preach.

I got out all of the scriptures I had studied and began to lay the Word of God on that little gathering. The one thing I had been taught well was that faith comes by hearing and hearing by the Word of God. So I quoted the scriptures on divine healing from Genesis to Revelation. I gave them my best shot.

When I was finally finished, I looked down at my watch and, to my surprise, I had spoken an hour and fifteen minutes. I looked at my brother

Neil in the front row who was obviously disturbed at having had to sit and listen to his little brother preach his first message for such a length of time. It had clearly taken a toll on his emotions, and he was not a happy man!

I told the people, as I had heard my former pastor do many times, that they should bring the sick the next night so we could pray for them and that they should come expecting the Lord to heal.

As we rode home on our bicycles, I was elated that God had filled me and enabled me to preach. Part of my question had been answered - now I knew that I could preach. My brother, however, was not so happy. In fact, he spent the entire trip muttering to himself - and to me - "If you ever do that again, if you ever make me sit and listen to you for an hour and fifteen minutes, I'll never come back!" and I couldn't say that I really blamed him. Neil was a year older and about my size. While he would have liked to have gotten into ministry himself, he was just too quiet and shy. Nevertheless, he was a great friend to me in those times and a strong supporter throughout my ministry.

When I woke up the next day though, the realization struck me that I had preached all I knew. I had covered all the healing scriptures in the Bible and really didn't have much else to say. You can imagine how I scrambled all day long trying to find another message to communicate to that little group of people.

As we approached the church on the second night I saw, to my amazement, that the place was

filled. It would only seat about fifty people but it
was packed and people were standing around the
outside of the building wanting to see this
American evangelist heal the sick. In fact, I was
sure all the people in Kingston, Jamaica were there
at the church.

I was excited, but scared as well. I realized that
God had given me the ability to preach the night
before, but would He answer my prayers for the
sick?

After giving a much shorter message I asked the
people if there was anybody there who was totally
deaf in one ear. This was how the evangelist always
did it so it had to work. If there was someone
totally deaf in one ear and God opened their ear
everybody would know it. If they could hear the
tick of a watch, hear a whisper, and demonstrate
their ability, faith would rise in the people for
further healing.

When I asked if there was anybody there who
was totally deaf in one ear there was complete
silence. No one moved. So I asked them again. No
one responded. All I could see was a room full of
white eyes in that country church with its kerosene
lamps.

I didn't have a "Plan B." This was all I had ever
seen my pastor do and it had always worked for
him. But of course he was preaching to thousands
and I was preaching to fifty. Apparently, there
were no deaf people in the congregation that night
at all, so I finally blurted out, "Is there anyone here
that, if God healed you, everyone would know it?"
I waited a moment and then a voice came from the

back of the building. A dear old black gentleman stood to his feet and said, "I've got a broken leg. If God heals it everybody will know."

I asked him to come down to the altar if he believed God would heal his broken leg, and he came down on a pair of crutches. I noticed, too, that he did not have a cast on his leg but it was wrapped with cloths. He was evidently a very poor man. I asked him if he believed that in Jesus' name God could heal his broken leg and he said, "Yes, I believe it!"

So I knelt down and the Lord and I had a personal encounter. Would God answer my prayer or should I go on back to Portland, Oregon, get a job and be the best member of my congregation I could be. I had nothing to lose so I prayed that God would do a creative miracle and instantly heal that man's leg.

When I was through praying everyone watched in dead silence. There was no soft organ music playing in the background. There was only my brother and me, and fifty pairs of eyes looking straight at me.

I took away his crutches and I said, "In Jesus' name, run down that aisle." He looked at me a little bewildered, wondering I'm sure, whether or not I knew what I had just asked. He turned slowly and with excruciating pain hobbled four or five steps without his crutches, then turned around and hobbled back to me.

I remember being a bit frustrated with him - I had told him to run and he was hobbling. So I told him again. "I said, in Jesus' name, run down that aisle!" And again he hobbled in pain a few steps down the aisle and then hobbled back.

This time I became angry. So I said loudly, "In the name of the Lord Jesus, run down that aisle, for God said He would confirm the word of His servant." And before I knew it that man turned around, took a leaping step and began to run down the aisle. Then he ran back to me. And then he began to leap and praise God with all his might for a notable miracle had been given us by the Lord.

Bedlam broke out in that church and I can't describe how excited I was. I now knew! Not only could I preach, but God would also confirm the word of His servant. I knew that I had been called by the Lord. There were no more doubts. And *that* was the beginning of my ministry.

Services went on every night for two weeks in that little Baptist Church and the Lord worked many miracles. As a result of those initial meetings, a Reverend Jones, the overseer of a group of independent holiness churches, invited me to minister in his churches. When the Bishop of the Church of God in Kingston heard what the Lord was beginning to do he asked me to preach in his churches as well. He, however, was upset when he found out I had already committed to Reverend Jones.

During this time, too, the Open Bible Church was preparing to plant their first church in Jamaica, in the city of Montego Bay. When they heard about my ministry they contacted me and asked me to be the opening evangelist at the crusade that would lead to the establishing of their first assembly. However, by that time I only had seven dollars to live on and Montego Bay was on the other side of the island from Kingston.

Prior to that invitation a very poor Jamaican man had come up to me in a meeting and said, "The Lord told me to give this to you" and he tried to hand me a one pound note. However, I refused to take it from him, but he kept pressing me. Finally I said, "OK, give me the money." And he gave it to me with great joy.

"Now you've obeyed the Lord and given me the money, haven't you?" I said. "Yes, sir," he replied at which point I put the pound note back in his hand and said, "Now, I want you to take it back." simply being unable to take the money from him.

The next day was when I received the invitation from the Open Bible Church. When I checked into the price of bus fare I found out it was exactly one pound. I didn't have that much money left, so I complained to the Lord,

> *It's always more blessed to give than to receive. But sometimes the Lord wants us to receive.*

"Lord, you've given me this opportunity and you haven't even provided for my bus fare." Then I remembered a voice saying over and over again, "The Lord told me . . . The Lord told me . . . The Lord told me."

I learned a valuable lesson that day. It's always more blessed to give than to receive, but sometimes the Lord wants us to receive. In fact, He puts us into a situation where we have to receive. If we refuse his provision in the name of pride, we will have missed his divinely chosen source for that time.

While the evangelistic team began a series of meetings in Cuba, my brother Neil and I received an invitation and a ticket from the Church of God to minister in the Bahamas. Again, the Lord was with us. The meetings hadn't lasted more than a

> *Sometimes you need to bend a little bit when it comes to nonessentials.*

few days when I received a knock on my motel room door and opened it to some of the elders of the church that had sponsored us.

They introduced themselves and then their chief spokesman, a very dark man in a white suit, stepped forward. "You know, we're a holiness church." he said. I nodded, saying I thought that was "good" and he continued. "We believe in living pure lives before God." he said.

"That's wonderful. That's great." I said, starting to wonder what they were getting at.

"We have some guidelines you need to agree with before you minister further." said another of the group - also dressed well and obviously another elder - stepping forward and handing me a five page list of do's and don'ts.

"OK, that's fine." I said reaching out to take it.

"We don't believe in wearing jewelry." the original spokesman blurted out.

"That's good." I agreed.

"So, we don't believe in wearing rings." he said rather shyly then, in a quieter voice and looking down.

I noticed one of the others eyeing the ring I had on my finger. It was a stainless steel ring I had made in high school. "It's hurting the faith of our people," the man who was staring said to which I responded by saying I was sorry immediately removing the ring from my finger.

So I learned as a nineteen year old preacher that to be effective you sometimes need to bend a little bit when it comes to nonessentials.

I held meetings all through the winter of 1949-50 for a total of five months. I preached and prayed for the sick and watched God save and heal many, many people. I had finally found myself in God, and I knew that He really loved me and cared for me. I knew that all the testings and trials of my childhood had only been preparing me for that day that God would thrust me out into the ministry.

I began to have a new and living faith in the Lord. I began to view God differently. The Lord began to enable me to overcome my inferiority complex, and an important part of this process involved memorizing several key scriptures that have stayed with me the rest of my life - such verses as:

> *I can do all things through Christ who strengthens me* (Philippians 4:13).

> *But my God shall supply all your need according to his riches in glory by Christ Jesus* (Philippians 4:19).

Nay, in all these things we are more than conquerors through him that loved us (Romans 8:37).

The LORD is my strength and my shield; my heart trusted in him, and I am helped: therefore my heart greatly rejoiceth; and with my song will I praise him (Psalm 28:7).

But he was wounded for our transgressions, he was bruised for our iniquities: the chastisement of our peace was upon him; and with his stripes we are healed (Isaiah 53:5).

These are the types of verses that you need in times of battle. They have been my stones.

During the time I was overseas in Jamaica and the Bahamas, Edie and I wrote to each other frequently, sharing the great things the Lord was doing in both of our lives. These letters and my ever growing love for Edie were a great source of strength.

I eventually rejoined the evangelistic party, including my parents, in Pennsylvania. Of course they were very pleased to hear of the way the Lord had blessed my ministry after leaving the main crusade. For my part, I knew that for the rest of my life I would handle God's Word and be a spokesman for Him. I knew I would believe Him for the impossible and see His hand move in miraculous ways. I knew there was no turning back.

In the process I had used most of my savings

but I did have enough money left to buy an old Ford taxicab, which I painted and drove all the way cross-country to Portland.

While I was in Jamaica though, I contracted hepatitis (or yellow jaundice as we called it then). It was embarrassing for the healing evangelist to return from a successful healing campaign sick. In fact, I was very sick. All I could do was lay around. I had no energy and I had gone down to 140 pounds. I remember walking over to my parents trailer and passing out - at which point my dad, a real man of faith, grabbed me and rebuked the sickness where upon, I felt hungry, having been instantly healed.

The joy of my life was marrying Edie Swanson on August 19, 1950. We had been engaged for over a year, and now the time had come to join our lives together. Having come through the good test of separation for the last nine months, our love was stronger than ever and we knew we were ordained for each other.

ॐ∘ॐ

At the time I had actually been away for the better part of two years - to Hanford and then to Jamaica - so essentially I was without a church. And, of course, Edie had been away in Canada. Earlier though, we once had attended a much enjoyed youth camp at Crystal Lake Gospel Park Church in Milwaukie, Oregon. It was a modern log cabin church set in a park amongst some giant fir trees - and it was there that my friend, Pastor Tom Fuller from McMinnville, married us. Edie's brother gave her away. Her friend sang, and her mother prepared a beautiful reception afterwards. My parents had wanted us to wait another year. Nevertheless they travelled back from Pennsylvania to be present. We had a beautiful wedding.

I traded my car for a little twenty-one foot trailer house that served as our first home. We lived in it for the first year of our married life, and although it didn't have any indoor plumbing, we were very happy just to be together. I also spent fifty dollars on a 1937 Chevy that burned as much oil as it did gas.

I borrowed a friend's Hudson, hooked it on to the trailer, and we took off on our honeymoon to Central Oregon. The car overheated going over the Santiam Pass so we spent the first night parked on a steep grade just a few feet off the highway feeling the trucks whizzing by all night. Afterwards, we parked by the Metolius River where we stayed for about a week. It didn't really matter where we were, or what had happened, we were that much in love.

During the fall of 1950, we traveled from place to place, preaching wherever God would open the door. God was with us and always met our needs. I was eligible for unemployment, but, to receive it, I needed to say I was looking for a job. I was so committed to the ministry by this time that I really wasn't looking for a job. Thus I refused the unemployment. Edie had a little bit of an inheritance from her Dad and even worked for awhile in a department store. I bought some old cars, fixed them and sold them for a profit. Though we got down to beans and cookies one time, the Lord always came through in the end.

During the whole month of October, we rented the armory building in Lebanon, Oregon and held meetings with my parents. Then, nine months after we were married - in April, 1951 - my father and mother were asked to pastor the little church we had attended in Portland before going overseas.

> *The Lord always came through in the end.*

During our absence the remainder of the congregation had withdrawn from the Pentecostal Church of God and become an independent congregation. They had decreased in size to such an extent that they were almost ready to close their doors, but before doing so they asked my parents to be their pastors. They accepted. The first Sunday we had thirteen people gathered around an oil stove in the corner of the church.

My father and mother did not have much actual preaching experience (my mother had the most experience in public speaking). However, they had always been great deacons and pillars in the church. They asked Edie and me to be co-pastors with them.

We accepted the charge and the four of us began to pastor Montavilla Tabernacle. Although I didn't know it at the time, I had reached another prophetic moment in my life. We soon changed the name of the church to Deliverance Tabernacle, relating to the healing ministry in which we had been involved. My father was the senior pastor, and I worked with him as the co-pastor. Of the first thirteen attendees, over half - including Edie's mom - were members of the Iverson family. In that humble beginning in 1951 was born what eventually would become known as Bible Temple.

We had reacted against the "wild fire" of the old pentecostal group and so our services were very dry. We had no praise, no clapping of hands, no emotional hype. We would just sing a few hymns and minister the word. It was only years later that the Lord led us into true worship, and, even to this day, I tend to react negatively to pentecostal, emotional hype.

This was a rather interesting time for us. Our hearts were still set on being missionary evangelists, but we were committed to being pastors. While we were working with a new congregation in Portland, we also were waiting for God to open the door for us to return to the West Indies.

It wasn't long before that door did open. In 1951, Edie and I drove all the way from Portland to Miami, then flew over to Jamaica to hold evangelistic healing crusades. This time, we held a series of meetings in the Church of God churches planning to stay until our money ran out. In fact, we spent most of that winter in Jamaica, going from place to place and from healing revival to healing revival, ministering and watching the Lord marvelously work with signs confirming His Word.

Edie was an attraction in Jamaica. She was a blonde and for that reason really stood out among the dark-skinned Jamaicans. In fact, they thought of her as a white healing angel. I want to say again and again that my wife has always been a woman of God and a woman of faith. She's always stood by me in a positive way throughout our entire lifetime and we've had some marvelous experiences growing together in the Lord.

Our first mission together overseas was no exception. We lived with the Jamaican people, and it was all new to Edie - the unsanitary conditions and food, the spiders, cockroaches and the banana leaf beds. Yet she readily adjusted to these conditions as I had done on my previous visit. She soon shared with me, too, a love for those people. The Jamaicans were so poor, yet they were always open and friendly. Never did we sense feelings of racism there. They never failed to make us feel wanted and special. Anytime they killed a chicken for us to eat - or gave us anything to eat for that matter - we always knew it was the best they had.

This is not to say that there couldn't be misunderstandings. I remember one time after a series of meetings when we noticed a tall handsome Jamaican women walking back and forth in front of the little house where we were staying. This went on for a couple of days, until finally, Edie and I went out to ask her what she wanted.

"You love me." she said, pointing to me, then repeated it, "You love me."

Taken aback and feeling somewhat awkward, and falsely accused with my wife standing there, I asked her what she meant.

"You healed my ears," she said, "so that I'm hearing. You love me."

Then she told Edie that Edie should go home

and find another man - because I'd healed her and she wanted to walk with me as my wife.

About the middle of our third month in Jamaica, we got a strong urgency from the Lord that we both had to go home. We were having a great time and could see no natural reasons why we should leave. When I told the bishop, he became very upset with me. In fact, when we arrived at the airport to depart, we were met by a trio from his church who turned their backs on us and

> *As long as we are in the will of God, the Lord watches over us and gives us the boldness of a lion.*

sang, "I Wonder Have I Done My Best For Jesus." Nevertheless, we remained committed to our plan for I knew no matter what the cost, it was essential to stay in the will of God. As long as we are in the will of God, the Lord watches over us and gives us the boldness of a lion.

In retrospect, we really were babies cutting our teeth in the ministry, on the island of Jamaica. I have always had a deep love both for the land of Jamaica as well as the Jamaicans themselves who allowed me an opportunity to minister when no one else would.

After arriving in Miami from Jamaica, we drove our car to Redding, Pennsylvania where we met with George Folk, the sponsor of the healing crusade that had taken place in that town two years earlier. While speaking with us in his office, George asked if I was ordained. I actually had never thought about ordination, but when he said he would be willing to ordain me right there with the Independent Assemblies of God, it seemed like a good opportunity so I agreed. He had me kneel down, then laid hands on me, prayed for me, and afterwards issued ordination papers. I walked out of his office an ordained minister.

We later drove to Detroit to visit the Bealls at Bethesda Missionary Temple. After that we drove home to Portland where we immediately found the reason for the Lord's urging us to leave Jamaica.

Awaiting me was a letter from the draft board informing me that I was being drafted into the army to fight in Korea. But, as it turned out, the Lord had other plans for my life, and His leading had circumvented the necessity. In one part of the notice I was asked for a possible basis for deferment. I simply wrote that I was ministering as an evangelist and mailed it in.

In a short while, I received a reply asking who had ordained me, how many ordained ministers were in the fellowship, and what I had been doing during the last three months that was connected to my ordination. Then I could see clearly why the Lord had moved me to return home early by way of Redding, Pennsylvania. I sent the report to the draft board, and they issued me the deferment. While at that point I didn't know what the Lord had in store for me, Korea was not a part of it, and Edie and I were grateful, curious, and relieved. On one hand my heart went out to the men in Korea who needed the Lord and to the chaplains ministering to them; and on the other I sought the Lord again for His will in my life.

Back in Portland, I continued to help my father pastor the new Deliverance Tabernacle doing much of the preaching through the early 1950's. All the while, I waited for God to open doors in the mission field.

God did open a new door for Edie and me in May of 1953, however, instead of the mission field, it was the door of parenthood. Our first child was born. Debra Ann Iverson would end up sharing some of our adventures, whether she wanted to or not.

D uring the summer of 1953, I became desperate for the Lord to show me clearly what He wanted me to do. I felt that it was something special but I didn't know what or where or when. My frustration led me to go on an extended fast to seek His mind.

❧

I took a little twelve foot trailer with just a bed and a table, and went up into the mountains along the Metolius River in Central Oregon. I told my wife I was not going to come back until I'd heard from God and I knew what He wanted me to do.

I clearly remember that time of prayer and fasting, the spiritual warfare I went through and the struggle to get into the presence of God. Finally a breakthrough came and I sensed the closeness of God in a way that I had never felt before. The word of the Lord began coming to me in a very clear way, and I began to write down things the Lord was speaking to me.

The first thing He said to me was that I was to go back to Portland and help my father care for His sheep which was the last thing I wanted to hear (what *I* wanted was to travel as an evangelist).

The Lord then spoke to me, however, that, within a year, I would be on foreign soil. I remember I'd brought a little globe with me and one day I gave it a spin and put my finger on it to stop it. Right above my finger was the island of Ireland, a place I didn't know anything about. I didn't even know if they spoke English there and actually didn't think that much more about it until later.

I finished the fast, went home and continued to work with my father as the Lord had instructed. Then, nearly nine months later, I received a letter from a friend of mine telling me that he had just returned from a series of meetings in Ireland. The moment I read it, my heart leapt, as I remembered the globe. Suddenly I knew where I was to go.

I immediately wrote to my friend and told him that I had a definite interest in Ireland and asked him if he knew of any contacts that I could make. He wrote back and gave me a list of a half dozen names. The first five were pastors of churches in Ireland where he had visited, and the last was that of a businessman in Ballymena.

I sat down and began to write to the pastors on the list but in each case - with each letter I attempted - I felt a strong check in my Spirit. In fact, I started writing to each of the five pastors and each time it was to no avail. I ended up throwing each letter away.

The only person that was left on the list was the businessman, Willy Davison of 40 Moate Road, Ballymena, so finally I began a letter to him:

"Dear Willy Davison," I introduced myself and said, "I would like to come to Ireland. I will be there a week from next Sunday and would like to hold revival services in Ballymena." This was probably the most foolish thing I ever did. I didn't know for sure why I was writing to him or what possibly could come of it. He didn't have a church, and I didn't know if he had any contacts; but I wrote to him and said I would be in Ballymena to hold meetings a week from Sunday. Somehow, in the simplicity of my faith, I honestly believed I was to tell him to expect me then and to plan on my holding meetings.

After I mailed the letter, I went to purchase a ticket. I said I wanted to be in Ireland by a week from Sunday, and the ticket agent just laughed at me saying there would be no way I could do that with such short notice. People in that day planned for months, and what few seats were available had all been booked. I said I would be willing to fly on stand-by, simply believing I was to be in Ireland a week from Sunday and that God would open a way. The agent said I was welcome to fly stand-by, but repeated that arriving in Ireland by the stated time was simply impossible. Also, he said, in order to reach Ireland in time through New York and Scotland even under the best of circumstances, I would have to leave by Wednesday night. That was assuming no delays - a seeming impossibility flying stand-by.

Nevertheless, on Sunday I told the congregation that I was going to go to Ireland. I explained how God had spoken to me and opened a door, and how I was going by faith. A good share of the congregation, small as it was, came to the airport to say goodbye, along with my wife and baby daughter whom I wouldn't be seeing for the next three months. I remember everyone standing in the Portland airport and saying goodbye to me, not knowing that I didn't even have a ticket.

Just a few minutes before the plane was to depart the public address system called my name and asked me to go to the ticket counter. When I got there, they said there had been a cancellation and I had a ticket to New York. I was thrilled to see God begin confirming His word.

I remember leaving Portland, looking down upon my city and thinking to myself, "What in the world am I doing? Where am I going? I'm going all alone to a country I've never been to, with no clear invitation and no guarantee that I can even get there." There had been no time to receive an answer back from Willy Davison and I was going strictly by faith.

When I landed in New York I went immediately to the airline counter to claim my reservation to Scotland - the one leg of my journey the agent in Portland had been able to confirm. However, somehow there had been a mix up and the ticket agent in New York never received word that I was coming. They were very apologetic but said there was no way I could be on the plane to Scotland. It was full and I *didn't* have a confirmed reservation.

I became desperate. I told them I had to be on the plane. I explained that I had to be in Ireland by Sunday and that there had to be a way. I told them I was going to sit on the floor and wait as long as it took to which came the now familiar response, "I'm sorry, sir, but there are no seats available." I did sit down in front of the lady at the counter though and for the next hour kept my eye on her. I would look at her and nod my head and she would shake her head back at me. Finally she got to the point that she wouldn't even look at me. I heard them announce the last call for the KLM flight to Scotland and I kept looking at her but she wouldn't look back. Then the plane engines started up and I heard the plane taxiing away from the gate where I was sitting. Then I heard the airplane take off. To make sure I walked up to the counter and asked if there was any space available yet; looking very sad she said, "I'm sorry, but the plane has already left."

There I was, sitting in New York City all by myself, wondering what in the world I was going to do. I was stunned! I was sure I would be on that plane. I was only obeying the Lord after all and now I thought He had left me stranded in another low point in my life.

This, however, was another of those "set times" - a time the Lord had chosen to work something new into my life and lead me down a new path. I sat down in front of the ticket counter, dazed and in shock. I prayed, "Lord, what am I going to do?" -

sitting there for probably five or ten minutes.

Then all of a sudden the girl at the ticket counter came running over to me and said, "Get your bags quick, there's a seat open on a Scandinavian Airline flight that's about to take off." I ran down the corridor with her to the Scandinavian Airline gate and within five minutes I was on board and on my way to Scotland. The Lord doesn't always accomplish His revealed will for our lives in the exact way we would like Him to, but He always succeeds in doing His will - in His time and in His unique way. The Lord is full of surprises.

On Saturday night, I landed in Prestwick, Scotland and had to change airplanes. I didn't

> *The Lord always succeeds in doing His will - in His time and in His unique way.*

have any time to lose. I had to get a connecting flight to Belfast right away. I went up to the counter and heard those same old words all over again. Of course, by then my faith level was so high I told them with confidence that there would be a cancellation and I'd be on the plane.

Sure enough, in a few minutes the announcement of the cancellation came and before I knew it, I was landing in Belfast, the night before I said I would begin my meetings. I took a taxi to a hotel not too far away from the airport and the next morning, Sunday morning, got up and took a train to Ballymena. I hadn't been formally invited; I didn't know if anyone knew I was coming, and I didn't know if anyone even wanted me to come.

All of a sudden I was quite afraid.

I got off the train in Ballymena and took a taxi to 40 Moate Road. I remember to this day standing there shaking in my boots as I knocked on the door with no clear idea of the reception I was going to get. The door opened and there stood a big, tall Irishman. I said, "I am Evangelist K. R. Iverson." With a huge smile he reached out and grabbed me, picked me up off the ground and began dancing around for joy. Needless to say, this was one reception I'd never anticipated. He said, "I received your letter and have rented the theater for special meetings. I sure was hoping you would come because I scheduled the meetings to start tonight."

With that, there began a love affair with the British Isles that to this day is deep in the spirit of our church. We have three sons in the faith pastoring in the U.K. and scores of others that we relate to and we thank God for what he did through that step of faith in 1954.

I must say that those were some of the most exciting times of my life as God opened doors of opportunity everywhere to preach the Word of God. I went home and brought my wife and baby daughter back with me to Ireland in January, 1955 and we spent an entire year ministering in that land. Hundreds of people came to know the Lord as we held healing revivals throughout Ireland and once in England.

Many times we would fill the town hall twice in an evening. Willy Davison worked with me as the song leader for two of those months, and another brother named Leslie Scott also ministered on our team. Debi was only 18 months old and the first half of the service I would hold her backstage while Edie led worship. Then, after taking the offering, Edie would take my place and I would go out to preach and pray with the sick.

It seemed like everything we did succeeded. Hundreds of people were saved and marvelous miracles took place. At times I was even shocked at some of the miracles. However, a few do stand out in my memory. Once - on my first trip to Ireland - a young couple, Tommy and Rita Wardle brought their eighteen month old daughter, Margaret, forward. She was the same age as our Debi, I remember, and had been born with a cleft palate. The Lord healed her and later, when Edie returned with me to Ireland, the Wardles became our dearest friends. Later they came to America and served as elders in our church. Margaret - who had been healed - came with her husband, too, and they served with us for ten years as elders, before returning home to Ireland where they now pastor a great church themselves. As Edie says, "the Lord has fit all the pieces together."

Another lady who was famous throughout Ireland and who I believe was in the Guiness book of records because she'd had twenty-eight children also came forward for prayer at one of our meetings. Her body was filled with tumors and she was dying. A week later she came back and interrupted the service, holding up the before and after x-rays showing she'd been completely healed. Her doctors had been confounded, she said, insisting on retaking the x-rays; and she and everyone who heard proclaimed the greatness of the Lord.

It was while in Ireland that I wrote my first book, *I Am The Lord That Healeth Thee,* and later a small booklet entitled *He That Believeth.* Little by little pride entered into my spirit. From the age of twenty-one, I had only known success in the ministry. I had never known a down side, never been in a desperate situation where I needed to call out to the Lord for help. Self-confidence rather than a humble dependence on the Lord was forming in my mind. The Lord needed to adjust me, and He did it in a most unique way.

I was told that Dublin had never experienced a real move of the Holy Spirit, that it was almost impossible to break into. Surely they could experience a revival through Dick Iverson, though! I made my plans and traveled to Dublin.

When I arrived in Dublin there was only one Pentecostal church and it was twenty miles out of town. Their vision was not to take the city but just to have a small "bless me club" and try to hang on until Jesus returned. I felt that if I identified myself with their group we would go nowhere. Therefore, as I had done in Northern Ireland, I

> *I had no vision for the local church - one of my main weaknesses at that time.*

bypassed the local church and went directly to the city. I had no vision for the local church - one of my main weaknesses at that time.

I was able to rent the Abbey Street Methodist Lecture Hall and I placed an ad in the Dublin newspaper, right on the front page, referring to myself as an "American Lecturer" being careful not to use the term "evangelist" which would have been against the local restrictions. I simply announced that I was going to lecture on the subject of "Divine Healing" and included some testimonies.

I had gained the cooperation of a few independent evangelicals in Dublin who believed in divine healing. In fact, some of them had loaned Edie and me the use of an apartment. However, this soon proved to be a negative rather than a positive.

The first thing I had scheduled was a showing of the film *Venture Into Faith* by Oral Roberts - a film which told the story of a young boy who had been a cripple but had been healed in one of the Roberts meetings.

My new evangelical friends called the Billy Graham headquarters to ask about Oral Roberts and received the report that Oral Roberts was extreme on tongues and healing and that he was Pentecostal.

I had never even brought up the subject of the Holy Spirit. My theme was divine healing. But when they found out I was Pentecostal, these evangelical brethren came to me and said that if I showed the film they would have to ask me to leave and that they didn't want any Pentecostal witness in their city. This was quite a blow to my plans. It was very difficult to find any short term accommodations in Dublin, but if I gave in to their demands, it would compromise my message. I refused and showed the film anyway.

The Lord then miraculously allowed us to rent a small apartment. In addition, while I had been able to rent the Abbey Street Lecture Hall initially for only one week, right after the film's showing, they said they would renew it if I wanted it for another week or two. We had a wonderful turn out for the film, and a number of people responded to the salvation call afterwards. That entire week was very successful. The crowds began to grow, and it looked as if we were going to have a move of the Holy Spirit in downtown Dublin regardless.

At the end of that first week when I went in to renew the rental contract for another week, to my chagrin they had changed again. They turned me down saying they had already rented it to somebody else. By then I had invested a lot of time and money in advertising and for rental of the auditorium and the apartment so I was counting heavily on the use of the hall.

In fact, I was nearly out of money by this time, and since I was not cooperating with any local churches, I had no outside support. Now the evangelicals *and* the Pentecostals were against me; I had no place to meet and no means to pursue any alternatives. I was frustrated and didn't know what to do.

No money. No support. No facilities. Nowhere to go, but just as I was about to despair, I received permission from the city to hold open air meetings in Dublin Park. This was simply never allowed and I looked at it as just another miracle provision of the Lord.

ৡৢ৵৹

I decided I would just have an outdoor evening meeting. I took a loud speaker into the park and began to preach in the open air. In the summer evenings there were a lot of people in the park so when they heard someone coming through over a loud speaker many came over and sat on the grass to listen.

Each night I preached and prayed for the sick who were there and the crowds began to grow. Soon several thousand people were gathering. This went on for about a week and was really gathering momentum.

However, on the next Sunday something unusual happened. In all the Catholic cathedrals in Dublin, the priests announced that the people were not to go out to Dublin Park and listen to the American evangelist preach. If they did, they would be guilty of a "mortal sin" and subject to eternal damnation.

Just prior to this time Tommy Hicks had turned the Catholic nation of Argentina upside down through a healing revival. With the fresh knowledge that a healing evangelist could bring such havoc, they simply decided to shut me down.

The next Sunday, I returned to preach in the park and instead of several thousand people gathering, there were only thirty-five people sitting around on the grass. I asked some of them what had happened and they told me about the stand of the local Catholic authorities - which was frustrating news to say the least. Still, as I look back on it, I can clearly see that God was just continuing to deal with me.

As time went on that summer no doors opened for me. Nobody responded to my ministry. No one reached out to us as a friend. We were simply all alone in Dublin, Ireland.

After several weeks of such isolation we were almost completely out of funds. We would get a little offering in the mail from time to time but never very much and we were literally living from day to day. It was a very scary time for us as we were seemingly stranded there in that foreign country - my wife, baby daughter and myself -

without even a ticket home.

Once again let me say that Edie has proven herself over and over again as a woman of great faith, and it was never more evident than during those difficult days in Dublin. She simply never would give into the devil's lie - that the Lord had forsaken us - but always believed the

> *If you're in the Lord's will . . . He will never forsake you.*

opposite, that ultimately the Lord would make it all right. "If you're in the Lord's will," she'd say to me, "He will never forsake you." At that point, despite her daily attempts to speak faith into my life the Lord was dealing with me and I wasn't hearing.

Edie loved Ireland. She loved being there, loved the lush green countryside and especially loved the people.

"I love it," she once said to me, "because it's right. What we're doing is right!" This was despite a terrific work load that fell to her there and the beginnings of her arthritis, caused, I believe, by the bone-chilling damp and cold. Not only did she have baby Debi to mother, but she led our song services, washed our clothes all by hand because there were no machines, ironed my clothes and those of three other team members who normally accompanied us, cooked four meals a day (including the one late at night after the last service) and washed the dishes as well.

"I was young, " she says, "and it was so right." Still, as we were leaving the port city of Cork, returning to America on the boat, the Lord spoke to her that she would not return to Ireland for a 'long, long time.' She didn't confide this to me until much later. I think because it hurt her so much. As it turned out, the Lord had a much different plan for us. In fact, Edie didn't get back to Ireland, the place she loved, for a whole twenty-five years.

While we were there in Dublin, as I've said, it was my turn to be down (we've noticed over the years that the Lord has seemingly arranged things and blessed us so that we've almost never both been down at the same time).

I remember writing home to my parents and asking them if the church would be able to send us some financial help. I didn't tell them how desperate our situation really was or that I was even running the risk of being deported. I thought that since I had ministered in the Portland church for a number of years without any financial remuneration they would automatically send us some help.

A couple of weeks went by before I received a reply from my dad saying, "I'm sorry son, but the church has just gone through a split and there are no finances to send you" (the congregation of one hundred had been reduced to about fifty-five).

After I recovered from the initial disappointment, I remembered I had one other source of money I could draw on. Before going to Ireland I had purchased a small piece of property on trade in an automobile sale and had told myself, if I ever got into trouble I could sell it. Now that I was in trouble I wrote to my oldest brother Morrie and asked him to please sell it, get whatever he could and send me the money. My hope was that he would get enough for our airfares home.

I waited optimistically for Morrie's letter, sure that the lot's sale was our solution only to be brought low by his reply two weeks later. He said that the lot I owned was worthless. It could not be developed, had been sold improperly to me and had very little value. In fact, the real estate company wouldn't even list it.

I could scarcely believe what I was reading. That lot, as I said, had represented security to me and now all my props were kicked out from under me. My family and I were *really* stranded and we had no way to get out of the situation. It stayed that way throughout the entire summer.

I was still going down to the park and preaching, just to have something to do. All the time I was hoping and praying that God would change our circumstances. One day

> *All my props were kicked out from under me.*

as we were driving down to the park to preach I decided to drive out onto the Dublin beach and let our two year old daughter, Debi, play in the sand. A year before I had purchased an American 1947 Ford. It was an obsolete car in the British Isles because it used so much gas. But it was big enough to pack all of our belongings, including baby furniture, and move from place to place. Then, too, I'd felt we just had to have some kind of car, the rule being if an American has a car, he still feels a certain amount of freedom.

Anyway, I drove out onto the beach to let Debi

play and in doing so got into some soft sand. I tried to get out of it, but then - and I remember that moment so clearly - the transmission went out. Needless to say, this was absolutely devastating - but the Lord used this turn of events as His moment of victory in my life.

I opened the door on the driver's side and literally fell out of the car onto the sand. I began to beat the sand with my fists and felt hot tears rolling down my cheeks. I said out loud, "I don't care anymore. If I'm deported it's your name, Lord, not mine. I don't care what you want to do with me."

I didn't know it at the time but the Lord was using my predicament to empty me of myself. I had come to the end of myself.

It seemed like I stayed there pounding the sand and weeping for nearly an hour. Then some Irish men came by and asked if I needed help getting my car out. I knew that low and reverse gears had been stripped, but that I still had second and high. Still the teeth that were torn out would be in the gear box and it would be just a matter of time before the rest of the transmission would be destroyed as a result. However, for the time being I had second and high gear, so I took them up on their offer.

> *The Lord was using my predicament to empty me of myself.*

I put it in neutral as they pushed, and sure enough, we were able to get out of the soft sand. I then limped the car, with my family, back to our apartment. I knew that at any moment the rest of the transmission could go out, but we made it back safely.

Something unplanned took place that night. We received an invitation to go to a friend's house for dinner. This was the only such invitation we had received all summer and the people arranged to have us picked up and taken to their home.

They sent a friend for us, an Englishman who was a Shell Oil Company executive. At that time, after World War II, there was some animosity between the British and the Americans, both claiming credit for victory in the war; and this Englishman was very British and very wealthy.

When we got into the car he said to me, "I hear you are one of those healing evangelists."

"Yes, sir, that's what I do." I said, " I minister to the sick and preach the gospel."

"I don't believe in that at all," he said very sarcastically. "I don't believe in the healing power of God."

Well, at that time I wasn't quite sure what I believed either! I told him, however, it was clearly taught in the Bible. This didn't impress him.

Soon we arrived at our friend's house and had dinner. Afterwards, he and I began a detailed discussion of the truth of divine healing. I shared with him my experience of God's power and authority that came as a result of faith in God, and after an hour or two of conversation I noticed there were tears coming down his cheeks. I asked him if he would like to give his life to Jesus, and he said he would. I had the privilege of leading that man to the Lord.

At the end of the evening he took me home and gave me an envelope as he dropped me off. In Ireland in those days, an average worker made five pounds a week and an offering of one pound was considered very generous. However, when Edie and I opened the envelope, we were amazed to see he had given us twenty pounds - a very large sum of money, especially considering we were completely broke.

The next morning I walked three or four blocks through the Irish suburb, not necessarily admiring the picturesque little brick bungalows - or "flats" as they were called - but intent upon getting the car fixed. I reached the neighborhood garage, a sort of humble home grown business, probably started there by the owner's father, and asked the owner, a short, red faced Irishman with a brogue, if he had an American 1947 Ford transmission in his wrecking yard. He simply laughed in my face and said no one in Ireland would ever preserve parts off that type of car - they were only good for junk.

Determined, I asked if there were any other wrecking yards in the area. He said there was one, so I asked if he wouldn't at least give them a call. He again laughed but then agreed to call, even though he continued to say it was hopeless.

He called the yard which was in downtown Dublin and asked if they had the part. When they said they didn't, instead of immediately hanging up the phone, he put his hand over the mouthpiece while relaying the word to me. "They don't have one" he said. Not knowing what else to do I asked him to ask again. The man on the other end again replied that he didn't have it; and again instead of hanging up the phone, my man held his hand over the receiver and repeated "sorry no American 1947 Ford transmissions."

I was a little hesitant, but finally said, "Okay, thank you." At that moment from the other end came the sudden news: "Wait a minute. You won't believe it but some men are dragging an American 1947 Ford through the gate right now! I don't know if the transmission is any good but we'll see." Well, when I heard that I knew without a doubt that the transmission was perfect - clearly God had arranged that moment. Without asking for a confirmation of the condition of the transmission, I asked him how much they wanted for it, and the answer was ten pounds. Then I asked the mechanic how much he would want to take out my old transmission and put in the new one - another ten pounds. This, of course, represented the twenty pounds I'd just received the night before. The Lord had wonderfully provided for the repair of our car.

We still needed some money to live on, but I had some of my books consigned in Armagh in Northern Ireland. I called Sally Morrison of the Armagh Christian Bookstore to ask her if there was any way she could just buy my books rather than leaving them on consignment. She graciously said she would and sent me sixty pounds for all of them. While I didn't have enough money to buy our tickets home yet, at least now we were able to get out of Dublin. Much more importantly, my faith and confidence had been restored!

I took out a map of Ireland and said, "Lord,

show me where you want me to go." It seemed as though my mind was drawn to a place called Enniskillen, County Fermanagh. So we drove to Enniskillen and held meetings in several small halls until we finally rented an empty wood product factory. The Lord began to move mightily by His Spirit and the meetings gathered momentum. According to the newspaper account, three to four thousand people gathered in one meeting - which was one of the greatest meetings in Ireland. Over eight hundred people were personally led to the Lord Jesus Christ and miracle after miracle took place.

In fact, the meetings were going so well that when our visa ran out I applied for an extension so we could continue. Unfortunately, all they would give us was a seven day extension stamped: *No Employment, Paid or Unpaid.* They told me I couldn't even *pray* since my work was that of a healing evangelist. My appeal of the ruling was denied and it was then that I learned that the Church of England had blackballed me because of the meetings' success. In this way they were forcing us out of the country.

> *The Lord began to move mightily by His Spirit and the meetings gathered momentum.*

The officials said that they would arrest me if I did attempt to pray for anyone. When my supporters heard that, in true Irish fashion, they told the officials that if they tried to arrest me there would be a brawl. Obviously I didn't want a brawl. However, I still felt strongly that our meetings should continue.

At this time, I remembered that Oral Roberts was ministering in Northern Ireland by means of radio, and I got an idea - what if I were to cross the border into the Republic of Ireland, tape a message, return to Northern Ireland and play the tape at the meeting? There didn't seem to be any way the officials could consider that a violation of my visa extension. I went to the police department and told them of my plan which they grudgingly approved.

Many wondered whether or not the crowds would hold under those circumstances - amazingly they increased! I'd sit on the platform and play the tape, then at the end would play a recorded altar call. Afterwards, I'd pause the tape and an assistant would step up and lead those responding in a sinner's prayer. Later I would turn the tape back on and play an announcement that I was now going to pray for the sick. The tape asked those who were sick to lay their hands on the part of their body that was sick while I prayed. And would you believe it? Many people were healed! We did this for five nights. On each occasion, the Lord marvelously met us.

We left Ireland in 1955 intending to return and hold evangelistic meetings again as soon as possible. Little did we know that it wasn't going to be that simple. We went home with the Lord having put our finances back in order - with a thousand dollars left over to buy a much needed car. There were other mountains ahead and other surprising turns in the road.

CHAPTER 7

In retrospect our time together in Ireland was so important to Edie and me and had life long implications, not just in terms of our ministering there and later through Bible Temple, but also in shaping our relationship and in building our own family.

ཨ་ཀྲ

During the lean times in Dublin - what Edie calls my "my dark and humbling period" - I learned a principle that would sustain and strengthen me many times in the future. The thing that got me through - that allowed me to maintain my sanity - was not the memories of the great miracles we had seen performed but was the times I spent making a fool of myself down on the floor with little Debi. At the time I thought I was just playing with her, but after a while I realized this was "daddy's therapy." This was so important too, because it underscored for me one of the most important lessons a pastor can ever learn. Your family is vitally important - more important than your ministry; and without a healthy nurturing relationship with your family, your ministry will neither thrive nor last. I've seen more than a few pastors with the "I'm in the ministry - my wife will take care of the kids" attitude; this rationalization

> *Without a healthy, nurturing relationship with your family, your ministry will neither thrive nor last.*

for neglect inevitably leads to disaster.

Fortunately, the therapeutic sessions I spent on the floor with Debi transformed my mind. Later on in other circumstances, because I had made it a mission to minister to my family, I was able to draw needed strength from them.

It's always seemed funny to me and its perhaps a window on our Lord's sense of humor that He saw fit to give me four wonderful daughters and no sons. After all, I came from an all boy family and had gone to an all boy's high school. Edie claims to this day that it was the Lord's way of completing my education and notes. Since the girls always preferred to go shopping with their mom, I have had Saturdays free to study whereas, if we had had boys, my time would have been taken up with baseball games and the like.

At any rate, the result was to keep me humble and tuned into the Lord - as in reality I had no idea how to raise the girls. When I did feel like going out and playing baseball, they would want to curl my hair! Consequently, I had to turn every day to the Lord for directions on how to father them properly. As it evolved, He showed me how to win their trust early - by spending quality time with each of them - so that later on they would confide in me and I could be their coach in such important issues as who my son-in-laws were going to be.

The ultimate effect of all of this was that, without my necessarily realizing it, my experiences with my four daughters gave me an understanding heart for all young girls and their problems. Over the years, Edie and I have taken in thirteen different girls into our home - some of them living with us for several years.

Our journey through life with its succession of prophetic moments usually involves relationships with special people the Lord brings to us. Edie was the first and most important such relationship for me. But the Lord was also bringing me (albeit at that point unwillingly) to a congregation that would dominate the rest of my life.

> *Our journey through life with its succession of prophetic moments usually involves relationships with special people the Lord brings to us.*

In January of 1956 we arrived home from Ireland in Portland, Oregon. Before really settling in, I made a three month visit to Cuba with my dad. In fact, Edie and I had been back in Portland for only month when I asked Dad to go with me. We started out by riding a bus to Miami, a trip which in itself took seven days and nights and a toll on my dad.

During the first week of meetings in Cuba, Dad had a gall bladder attack and had to return home after an extended stay in Florida. This was the beginning of the loss of his health. I remained in Cuba for three months, working with a Cuban brother, Raul Trujillo to open avenues into the Latin community which later would prove important.

In my absence, the strain on Edie back in Portland was extreme. Our little Debi came down with a terrible case of bronchitis, and Edie later confided that often in the night, when Debi would be wheezing and coughing and gasping for breath, Edie would be beside herself, wondering if her next breath might be her last. It wore on Edie terribly, not having me there as her covering and to pray for Debi. I think it was difficult, too, because Edie so recently had been with me heart and soul in the mission field and now, because of financial considerations, had to stay behind.

After I returned home to Portland, Edie and I held a few evangelistic meetings in the area. Dad and Mom pastored the church, but from that point on I did most of the preaching.

I also got involved in business. In fact, my brothers and I ended up owning a car lot in Southeast Portland called Iverson's Auto Mart. I would travel a route buying cars at a wholesale rate and then sell them retail on our lot or whole sale them at a dealer auction. I was the buyer, Morrie was the retailer and Neil was the mechanic. This involvement with business gave me some knowledge about finances and administration which would prove valuable as time went on.

On January 12, 1957, our second daughter, Diane, was born. She was the joy of our lives during a very frustrating time. Dad and Mom were trying to have a "revival center" and were having evangelists come through whenever possible, but the services were very shallow. Some of the evangelists were charlatans, and we were experiencing a lot of tension over it with my parents. At that point, my family and my business were the bright spots in my life.

In early 1959, we had a series of revival services with visiting husband and wife evangelists and our little church was packed out week after week, for thirteen weeks. We thought we were taking the city by storm. We had only about one hundred members but the services were running around two hundred, which was at or near the seating capacity of our building.

It was at this time we attempted to rent the Granada Theater on the corner of 76th and Glisan, just a few blocks from our church. It would seat six hundred and fifty people, enabling us to continue our sudden growth.

The theater had been shut down for over two years but when we contacted the owners they indicated they wanted to sell, not rent the theater. Since we only wanted to rent it, we were at an immediate impasse.

In June, while on my auto buying route in Pendleton, Oregon, the Lord awakened me in my motel room, He spoke to me out of Nehemiah chapter seven. In fact, He spoke several things to me out of that scripture that would set the course for what eventually would become known as Bible Temple. I didn't use correct hermeneutical principles to gain these insights; it was simply one of those unique prophetic moments the Lord brought into my life. Nehemiah chapter seven says:

"Now it came to pass, when the wall was built, and I had set up the doors, and the porters and the singers and the Levites were appointed. That I gave my brother Hanani, and Hananiah the ruler of the palace, charge over Jerusalem: for he was a faithful man, and feared God above many. And I said unto them, let not the gates of Jerusalem be opened until the sun be hot; and while they stand by, let them shut the doors and bar them; and appoint watches of the inhabitants of Jerusalem, every one in his watch, and every one to be over against his house. Now the city was large and great: but the people were few there in, and the houses were not builded. And my God put into my heart to gather together the nobles and the rulers and the people that they might be reckoned by genealogy." (Nehemiah 7:1-5).

From this it was absolutely clear to me and I knew that the Holy Spirit had said that we were to buy the theater and that God was going to pour out His Holy Spirit there. Just as Noah had prepared the ark before the rain came, the rain of the Spirit would come to us after we prepared our new gathering place.

Also, I believed, after this encounter, that we were no longer to have a congregational form of church government but that we were to appoint rather than vote in our elders. I also believed that my dad and I were to continue as the leaders, that we were to fix the building and be in it before the summer was out, and that for a long while the building would be large but the congregation would be small.

Further, when I read Nehemiah 7:8, that *"the children of Parosh (numbered) two thousand one hundred seventy and two,"* I felt the Lord might be saying our congregation eventually would number over two thousand - though I didn't quite have enough faith for that and for the time, at least, put that word on the shelf.

My father was still the senior pastor at Deliverance Tabernacle but he was laying in the hospital recovering from his first heart attack when all these things began to take place. I went to his hospital room and very carefully told him that I thought the Lord wanted us to purchase the Granada Theater in order to prepare for a move of the Holy Spirit. My father's words were, "Son, if He has spoken to you to buy the theater, then that is what we should do." I was actually surprised at his response because he had poured his life into the little church building on 80th and Washington, and it really was his life. His walking away from it was proof in my mind that the Lord had already dealt with him.

On the other hand, the purchase of the

Granada Theater was one of the key moments in my life. We didn't have a large congregation but we believed that there was going to be a move of the Holy Spirit. I remember bringing our small flock to show them the old theater. I turned the lights down low so all the flaws wouldn't be visible. They agreed with me to buy the building for $33,000. We were able to raise $13,000 and when I tried to borrow the balance from the bank, they were unwilling to loan money to a church, especially to an independent church with no denominational fellowship backing them up. If the bank had to foreclose on a church, it would be poor publicity in the community. In addition, theaters are not multiple use buildings and are considered a poor investment. Bank after bank turned us down.

> *The purchase of the Granada Theater was one of the key moments in my life.*

Then something strange happened. A year prior to this I had invested $500 in the start up of a new insurance company which was the only time I had ever bought any stock. A Christian woman talked me into buying it, but later I thought I had made a mistake. Little did I know the Lord was going to use that investment for His glory.

I began to wonder what insurance companies do with their money. Then I remembered that they loaned money. So I went to the company office, walked in the door, stopped at the counter and said, "I'm a stock holder and I'd like to see someone about a loan." Well, even though they didn't know how much stock I owned, because I was a stock holder I gained immediate access to the officers of the company. After all, the main officers are voted in by the stock holders.

Without any appointment, I found myself sitting across the desk from the vice president. He happened to be a backslidden Foursquare man who knew Amy Semple McPherson personally. I had immediate rapport with him, but he also indicated that the chances of an independent church borrowing money to purchase a theater were remote. He told me he couldn't make the decision himself and that only the president would be able to do so. I asked if I could see the president.

He immediately picked up his phone and called the office of the president. It was about noon by this time. Nevertheless, within a few minutes, the president of the insurance company came into the office, a dignified gentleman in his sixties. After the usual introductions, I told him our church wanted to apply for a loan on a theater we were purchasing for a sanctuary. I could tell he wasn't too impressed with my plan, yet he obviously felt the need to be courteous, knowing I was a stock holder. He first let me know he was committed to protecting my investment, then pointed out that loaning money to a church was not the best way to do that.

I asked if he would at least look at the building before he made his final decision. That put him on the spot since I was not asking for any kind of immediate commitment. Grudgingly, he said he'd look at it but that it definitely wasn't the kind of investment they were interested in making.

Looking at his watch he said, "Let's look at it right now."

Within twenty minutes of the time I had walked into the insurance company office, I found myself in the automobile of the company president on the way to 76th & Glisan to look at our broken down building. During the ride in the car I tried to carry on some conversation, but it was only one way. I think he resented being put on the spot. He was also probably wondering how much stock I owned and whether or not all this inconvenient courtesy was worth it.

The old theater had been abandoned for over two years. Vandals had gotten in and torn up the entire inside and the roof leaked so it was quite musty and smelly. When we arrived, I told the company president to wait just a moment so I could go in and turn on the lights. As before, I turned them on very low so he couldn't see all the water marks and stains.

"Who in the world would want to have a church in this place?"

I brought him in and began to paint a picture of how we were going to fix up the building and make it look good. The president said nothing, but I could sense that he was thinking, "Who in the world would want to have a church in this place?"

After looking around for a few minutes he pointed to a stairway asking, where it led. I responded that it led to the projection booth. Before I knew it he started up the stairs. We squeezed into the old booth and noticed that all the projectors were still there. They must have been fifty years old - real antiques.

Beer cans and various other junk had been strewn on the floor by the vandals, but there was also old film scattered about as well. My executive companion, who said he'd never been in a projection booth before was intrigued by both the projectors and the film.

Some of the film was maybe thirty years old. He picked up a piece of it off the floor and held it up to the 40 watt bulb. And wouldn't you know it? He had seen that particular movie! He began to look at the film frame by frame, holding it up and saying "I remember this scene!" or "I remember this person!"

I stood there in amazement, watching this dignified sixty year old executive turn into a little child. Suddenly I understood what God was doing. For the next hour he and I played together in that room. I knew the Lord was taking this stiff, starchy executive and making him pliable and responsive, willing to do something he would not ordinarily do. We tried to figure out how to thread the film through the projector. We played with all the pieces of equipment in the room until our hands were covered with dirty dust from the film.

Finally, he said he thought it was time to go.

We walked down the musty stairs into the auditorium. He looked out over the audi-

> *"I can see how this would make a wonderful church."*

torium, still dimly lit, still stained and musty, and he said, "I can see how this would make a wonderful church." God *had* molded and changed his heart.

We walked out to his car and the executive mask came back down over his face. He turned to me and said, "We do have a problem, though." My heart sank. I asked him what that might be, and he answered that it would be at least two weeks before he would have the money to lend us. I tried to remain calm as I replied, "I think that'll be okay. We can wait two weeks."

Thus the Lord marvelously gave us the opportunity, with a handful of people and the insurance company's help, to buy the Granada Theater. We were off and running on the next leg of our journey.

Wh e were now ready for a great visitation. In fact, we were so excited we changed the name of the church from Deliverance Tabernacle to Deliverance Temple in anticipation of a harvest. The Lord had revealed to us that if we bought an auditorium that seated six hundred and fifty people, even though we had only one hundred, He would pour His Spirit out on us. We had obeyed the Lord and He had marvelously enabled us to buy the theater.

᠍᠍᠍

᠍᠍

However, our sense of timing is almost never the same as the Lord's. The timing of the Lord's will is under His sovereign control. And correct timing is everything.

We bought the old theater in June and immediately went to work remodeling it. It was in such bad shape that we weren't able to finish the basic repairs until October. You remember the Lord had spoken to me out of Nehemiah: *Let not the gates of Jerusalem be opened until the sun be hot.* I took that to mean it would still be hot when we moved into the new building. It's rarely hot in October in Oregon. However, in the year of 1959, we had a rare Indian Summer and it was very hot in October. Even that seemed to be a confirmation of the Lord's will.

In the fall of 1959 we were ready to welcome the evangelist who had been with us earlier in the year - returning for meetings that would surely result in a move of the Spirit and the filling of our new sanctuary. During the summer we had heard a rumor that this evangelist and his wife were unhappy with the offerings we had given them. We had also heard they were planning to start their own church in Portland. Before starting the latest meetings we asked them, however, and they declared that both stories were untrue. In fact they agreed to state so publicly at the first service.

We began services with a great spirit of faith and expectation. The meetings went on for a solid month, the results were not even what we'd seen early in the year. We had between two and three hundred on Sundays and even fewer during the week.

After a month of this, I told the evangelist that on the next Sunday we would announce there would be only one more week of services. And to make a long, unfortunate story short, the evangelist and his wife really were plotting against us.

Incredible as it now seems, that Sunday when I tried to announce the coming end to the meetings, the wife disrupted the service. In the end there was a church split and half of our congregation defected to a theater the evangelist had rented across town.

Now we had a big theater and a small, split church. To be honest, our church had grown from one to two hundred as a result of the earlier meetings, so the one hundred that split from us were there because of the evangelist anyway. However, some of those who had been with Dad from the beginning left as well, and Dad never got over that hurt.

That church split turned out to be a good thing for me, though, and for our congregation. It woke me up from my naivete and it also cleaned the house of the "sign-seekers."

Now we were a small group of one hundred again, occupying just a few seats in that old theater. In fact, for a time we were probably the only church with a tavern in our facility. Rita's Tavern had a lease with the old owners which we inherited for a short time. When it was up, they wanted to continue our partnership of old wine and new wine; we, however, were ready for them to move on, and I was ready to move on too.

My father's heart had been seriously damaged by his first heart attack in late 1958. However, now I was really anxious to get back out on the evangelistic field where my success had been. I had never known anything but success as an evangelist, speaking often to thousands, and I certainly wasn't looking to stay home with a shrinking, discouraged congregation.

I had spent nearly ten years ministering as a healing evangelist, had traveled to many different countries, and had seen God bless our ministry with signs following. Many people had testified of miraculous healing and seeing God move in the supernatural is something that one doesn't forget.

At the beginning of 1960 we found out Edie was carrying twins. We were very excited and made all the preparations for their arrival. On July 25, Edie gave birth to two beautiful baby girls, whom we named Brenda and Angela. They were premature and weighed about five pounds each. Angela had a difficult time breathing and, while the doctors indicated that this was not unusual for premature babies, they definitely seemed concerned about the struggle she was having.

We went before the Lord and prayed that God would protect our child, that she would be a normal child. However, on the second morning following the birth the phone rang at four a.m. I answered the phone and it was the doctor who said, "Reverend, I'm sorry, but your baby is dead." This was a very dark moment. It was the middle of the night, but the night suddenly seemed to be much darker. I couldn't believe that death had invaded my home. I couldn't believe that God had allowed it to happen. And in the midst of the darkness I felt the spirit of faith slipping from my

> *To become faithless is one of the most horrible things that can happen to a person.*

soul.

To become faithless is one of the most horrible things that can happen to a person. I can testify to it because of what I experienced that night. I remember weeping and asking God why He would allow such a thing - why He would allow my baby to die. I was a healing evangelist. I'd prayed for children all over the world and He had answered my prayers for them, but now He refused to answer my request to heal my own child. As a healing evangelist I had always taught that if I prayed for someone's baby and he wasn't healed it was not my fault, but rather there was something wrong with that person's faith. But now I had prayed for my own baby, and she had not been healed.

Night after night I found myself walking the floor shaking my fist in the face of God. "Why, God! Why would you allow this to happen to me?" I remember telling God I would not be His spokesman if He wouldn't hear me. I closed the Bible on my desk and told Him I would never preach the Word again. I said I would never be able to stand with confidence again and declare Him to be faithful when He had not been faithful to me. My spirit had reached its lowest ebb, and I fell into a dark abyss in my soul.

For weeks I wasn't able to get a hold of my emotions. I felt as though God had forsaken me, had failed me. And nothing anyone could say got through to me - including Edie who handled the whole thing better than I, and who, of course, had Angela's baby sister, Brenda, to look after as well. Even after the Lord spoke to me, I didn't really understand until later when some other pieces had fallen into place. I didn't comprehend that the loss of Angela was part of a process to give me understanding and empathy for the problems of others - i.e., to change me from an evangelist to a man with a pastor's heart.

I continued to wrestle with God, but finally, after six weeks of darkness, faithlessness, and hopelessness, He came to me in the night. "Death is an enemy, He said, "and you have had the enemy of death touch your life for the first time. The last enemy to be destroyed is death, which will be destroyed on My return." Then He quoted to me Genesis 3:15: *"And I will put enmity between you and the woman, and between your seed and her seed; he shall bruise your head, and you shall bruise his heel."* This Scripture says that the seed of the woman will crush the serpent's head, and that the serpent will bruise his heel. The Lord spoke to me that night and said, "Son, you had your heel bruised, but Angela herself is with me. You'll see her again and live with her for eternity. If you don't lose your faith in Me through this bruising of your heel, if you'll continue to trust me, I will allow you to crush the serpent's head."

Suddenly the deep darkness lifted from me and a bright light shown into my spirit.

When the Holy Spirit spoke that word into my heart that night, suddenly the deep darkness lifted from me and a bright light shown into my spirit. It almost felt like I had been drowning and could suddenly breath again. I remember, through my tears, saying, "Lord, I want to crush the enemy under my feet! If it's possible, let every soul I win to you from this day forward, be credited to the account of Angela."

The Holy Spirit came upon me that night and gave me fresh vision and direction for my life and ministry. More than ever, I understood the importance in life of never losing faith, hope and love. These are the three motivating forces God has put into the human spirit that empower us to overcome anything that might come our way.

Soon after the Lord had spoken these things to me, I was presented with an opportunity to return to Ireland on a three month evangelizing mission. Normally, I would have been absolutely thrilled, as it was what Edie and I had wanted for such a long time. However, I was really torn. With baby Brenda, Edie couldn't go - couldn't return to the place she so loved - and there was the added emotional burden of the fresh loss of Angela.

I wrestled with it but found myself in one of those seemingly unsolvable puzzles with which we are sometimes confronted. On the one hand I felt absolutely driven to go - to get out of the seemingly dead end confines of our little Portland church and get back to the evangelizing field where I thought I belonged. On the other, there was my commitment to family before ministry, and the belief that Edie needed me.

I was caught in a vise and it was serious. I felt the pressure mounting with the September departure date fast approaching, but then my great lady, Edie, totally surprised me on hearing of my opportunity.

"Dick, you have to go," she said "It's of the Lord." And while, at that point, neither of us understood why it was of the Lord - how He would use this trip to help settle me into the change He'd planned for my life - there was suddenly a peacefulness about my going. I knew that Edie would be all right. In fact, Edie confided that the Lord had spoken to her heart the previous year - before the twins had ever been conceived - that I would soon be going to Ireland without her. This explained her wonderful tranquility.

In September I left for Ireland, on a visit that would prove to be very disillusioning but also enlightening. Five years earlier, we'd had a great harvest. I had personally followed up on around eight hundred people, and I was looking forward to seeing many of them again as well as conducting new services.

I was shocked when only a few people came to the meetings. The harvest had been lost. I found out that as soon as we had departed, some very conservative evangelicals had visited the towns where we had been, distributing material condemning all things pentecostal, and of course, over half of the converts had been Roman Catholic.

To this day, it remains perhaps my greatest regret that I'd had no vision for the local church or for church planting. The memory of the hundreds of young men who were looking to me for direction in 1955 was a bitter lesson, but would also become a driving force later on at Bible Temple as we trained teams in our Bible college for work in the mission fields. I could have and should have trained those young Irish men to be pastors had I fully comprehended the importance of local churches; and, had I done so, much of that harvest would have been saved.

The Lord effected two other important changes in me during that trip to Ireland in 1960 - changes which didn't directly affect the Irish people, but which had wide if not thoroughly understood (at that point) implications for my life and for my transformation to pastor. One was that I found I just couldn't bear being away from my wife and our children for such a long stretch. I missed them terribly and wondered each day what each of them was doing. And then the Lord also spoke to me very plainly while I was there that on returning home I needed to give up my car business and focus totally on ministry. When I returned home, I had at least two pieces of news that Edie was glad to hear.

Still, I didn't quite get it. The Lord had prepared Edie's heart ahead of time to get me to Ireland by myself. He'd taken baby Angela from us to soften my heart. He'd caused me in Ireland to finally recognize the pre-eminent importance of the local church. He'd made me unbearably homesick and caused me to give up my business - a projected source of revenue for future overseas missions. Yet, I stubbornly clung to the belief that I was an evangelist and not called to our Portland church.

During the winter of 1960-61, my father had a second heart attack. At that time he said the doctor told him if he wanted to live any longer he would have to resign. And guess who he wanted to take over as the new Senior Pastor? I said, "Dad, I'm not called to be a pastor, I'm an evangelist." For, though the Lord had been changing me, I was still resisting.

Dad said he wasn't willing to turn the church over to anyone else, and would continue to pastor if I wouldn't take it. When I talked to the doctor myself he told me if I didn't get my father away from the pressures of the church the next heart attack would kill him. This, of course, put me in another dilemma. As I said, I was still looking forward to success as an evangelist, and I thought that the last thing I wanted was to take responsibility for a split church with a hundred people and a big auditorium that still needed a great amount of work. On the other hand, if I didn't take the church and my father died with a heart attack, then I would have that on my conscience the rest of my life.

It was a very hard decision to make, but finally I decided to resign - decided that my life was separate from his and that I needed to live it. I gave Dad my letter of resignation to read at the next board meeting but when we got to the meeting he gave it back to me, saying I should read it. I opened the envelope and began to read, but instead of my letter, I found myself reading a letter of resignation from Dad and Mom. Somehow I knew then that it was right and I told my father I would take the church.

I told him I wanted him and Mom to take off and travel and get out from under the pressure -

which made him so happy he made plans with my mother immediately to go to Mexico to work as missionaries.   On January 29, 1961, this was announced to the church along with the big news that Mr. and Mrs. K.R. Iverson would assume the pastorate of the church.

Actually my real plan was that as soon as my parents left town, I'd hand the church over to the first preacher who walked through our doors.   In fact, if I found out a preacher was visiting during a Sunday morning service I'd invite him to preach that night, hoping he would prove to be a candidate to take the church.

The problem with my scheme was that I had too much integrity to just turn the church over to a minister who was not honest and upright, and the only preachers who seemed to come to us in those days had major problems.   They all turned out to be either immoral or charlatans, after money or involved in gimmickry.

I can't tell you how frustrating a time this was for Edie and me.   All I wanted was to get out and no matter how hard I tried, I couldn't seem to escape pastoring that little church.   I just

I waited - somehow not recognizing that God was putting me through His own school.

knew the world was waiting for the revelations of Dick Iverson, when all the while I was held captive to a handful of people with no real appreciation for my gifts.

So I waited and I waited and I waited - somehow not recognizing that God was putting me through

His own school. For example:

One morning I sat up in bed at two o'clock, completely awake. I heard a voice within in me say, "Get up!" So I got up. The voice then said, "Get dressed!" So I put my trousers on. The voice said, "Go, get in your car!" So I did.

As I came to the first main road a half a block from my house, the voice said, "Turn left." Ordinarily I would have turned right at that intersection and you can imagine how I felt. Here I was in the middle of the night following this inner voice and I had no idea where I was going.

About five blocks away I came upon a mobile home park and the voice instructed me to turn in. At this point, I remembered there was a young single mother living there who had gotten saved in our church. I know this sounds a little suspect but I had absolutely no interest in going to her house. All I was doing was following this inner voice. I drove by her trailer noticing that everything was dark, then I drove to the end of the trailer park, turned around and came up the other side.

While I was turning, it felt like two hands were placed on my face to turn my head. I looked over my shoulder and there, out in a field, was a telephone pole with a light at the top and underneath, a car. The car looked a lot like one I had recently sold to a visiting preacher. This particular man had an excellent ministry, so good that I really was about to turn the church over to him. In fact, Edie and I were preparing to leave in a couple of days for a vacation and, if everything went well while I was gone, I was going to give him the church when we returned. Then at last I could be off to the evangelistic field!

Well, I simply couldn't believe it was his car. He was a married man so why would his car be parked at this trailer park?   I knew he was familiar with this single mom, but I just didn't want to face the possibility that something was going on between them.   I took down the license plate number and then went home and back to bed.

> *The Lord loved His church so much that He supernaturally protected it from my folly.*

I didn't tell Edie what had happened. I checked the license plate number of the car though and, sure enough, it was his. I thought to myself that maybe he just had car problems and left his car there in the field. But during the day, when I drove back by, the car was gone.

The next night - on my own - I got up at two o'clock and drove over to the trailer park; and the car was back. When I confronted him the next day he confessed. Even though I just wanted out, the Lord loved His church so much that He supernaturally protected it from my folly.

A year of extreme frustration followed. I was becoming increasingly more desperate as it was growing clearer and clearer that I wouldn't be able to escape my father's sheep. What did the Lord want me to do with them? I figured I had better find out. In this time of frustratration, although I didn't know it, I was hungry for more of the Lord.

One of my greatest disappointments that first year was the rejection of my ministry by my pentecostal brethren in Portland.   As a senior pastor I wanted to identify with a fellowship larger than ourself so, I contacted the local pentecostal ministers association and asked to be a part of them.

I remember when an Oral Roberts crusade was scheduled.   I wanted to be involved but I was informed that because we were a "latter rain" church, we couldn't be accepted. This was strange because, not only was I not "latter rain," but I didn't even know what it was.

Consequently, I was only able to get together with about five small, independent pentecostal churches in town. Most of our fellowship had to come from outside of Portland.

I n January of 1962, I decided to take my children out of school, purchase a travel trailer, and take a five week vacation. I was determined to visit every church I could find along the way because I wanted to see what God was doing. I'd heard He was moving here and there, but I knew He wasn't moving in any particular way in Portland.

❧

So Edie and I and the kids started out on a five week pilgrimage, and, as I said, we tried to find a church service in every town we came to, even if it wasn't Pentecostal.

As I touched on earlier, the year I went away from home to work at the atomic energy plant in Hanford, Edie attended several services at a little church in Portland called the "Wings of Healing." Several pastors were there ministering - from North Battleford, Canada where there was a great new outpouring which became known as the "latter rain."

Edie was so inspired by these services that the following year she decided to go to North Battleford to attend Bible college. I was evangelizing in Jamaica at the time. In letters we exchanged, she would describe what was happening and tell about the "heavenly choir."

The "latter rain" movement, as I have mentioned, was characterized by the Holy Spirits' emphasis on prophecy and the laying on of hands, as well as the "sacrifice of praise" form of worship to which Edie kept alluding. However, as with many other movements or outpourings of the Spirit, there came afterwards distortion and fakery. Charlatans got a hold of it and all sorts of offshoots went spinning off out of control. In many church circles the "latter rain" became known as the "scattered rain" and was roundly ridiculed. Just the mere rumor that our church might be a part of it was enough to bar our participation in the pentecostal ministers' association. In the beginning, when Edie had sent letters about this movement, I had been open to it. Over time, however, things had changed and I had come to see more of the charlatans than of the good.

That's why what followed was all the more amazing and I can only praise the Lord for it and for my wife who never forgot what she'd seen and heard and didn't fail to persevere in her persuasion.

As we pursued our pilgrimage to various churches, Edie was eager that we visit two churches in particular pastored by two men she'd seen minister in Canada - David Schoch and Reg Layzell. These churches were in Long Beach, California and Vancouver, British Columbia respectively. To this day, I thank the Lord that I agreed.

My first encounter with David Schoch was, in fact, one of those key prophetic moments in my life--in more ways than one. Brother Schoch was not only a pastor, he was a prophet.

I still remember being with my family in his church in Long Beach, California for the first time. Bethany Chapel was an older, traditional building which seated about four hundred. The auditorium was packed and, as the worship service began, the presence of the Lord was especially powerful. Being raised in a Pentecostal church, I had heard praise before, but this was different. They *worshiped* the Lord by lifting their voices and singing praises to Him, spontaneously, both in known and unknown languages.

At first I thought it was tremendous, but only for a short while. Soon I found myself becoming agitated. In fact, I became so agitated I wished that they would stop. I had never experienced prolonged praise before, and it just went on and on. After a time, the spontaneous season of worship died down, and several prophecies were given. Then a great volume of praise began again. I remember shifting from one foot to the other, waiting for it to finish, eventually realizing that maybe it wasn't going to end for a while. In my irritation, I began to judge the church and criticize its unusual worship.

At that point the Holy Spirit spoke to me and said, "What's wrong with what they're doing?" I replied, "Nothing is wrong. They're lifting their hands, singing, and worshiping the Lord." Then the Spirit said to me, "Why don't you do it too?"

So I lifted my hands and joined in singing love songs to the Lord. For the first time I *really* worshiped Him. The "fountains of the deep" in my spirit broke loose. The heavens opened, and I found myself in the presence of the Lord in a way I had not experienced before.

> *The "fountains of the deep" in my spirit broke loose. The heavens opened, and I found myself in the presence of the Lord in a way I had not experienced before.*

The service lasted for over two hours, though Pastor Schoch preached for only about twenty minutes. I thought if I ever had such a move of God as I experienced in their worship time, I'd not think to preach at all. In fact, at the end of the service I just wanted to get alone as quickly as possible so I could think and pray about what I'd just been in. It was one of the most moving experiences I'd ever had.

On the way out of the church I saw Brother Schoch standing in the traditional place by the door, shaking hands with those who were leaving. He was a short, stocky, German fireball of a preacher who operated with great emotion, but who also was a renowned prophet. Knowing that he would probably recognize our family as new, I thought that as soon as I told him I was just visiting from Portland, Oregon, he wouldn't bother me anymore. I was wrong.

After we shook hands, and I told him we were from Portland, he asked what church we attended. I said we went to Deliverance Temple. He looked strangely in my eyes then asked, who the pastor was. I was trapped and had to identify myself.

He asked if we would like to have lunch with him, and, though I was honored, I really just wanted to disappear as quickly as possible so I could think over what had happened. However, there was no escaping, and thus began a relationship with David Schoch that continues to this day, a relationship that has proven to be as important as any I have ever had.

We went to lunch in a nearby restaurant and I was still mesmerized by what had taken place. In our church, one out of eight Sundays we might have a decent service, with the other seven being bone dry. So, I asked Pastor Schoch, as we sat with him , if the service that day had been typical and his un-emotional answer was that it had. When I asked him why he felt it necessary to preach after such a prolonged and powerful move of the Spirit his answer became more animated, even argumentative.

> *"Wherever there's a spiritual move," he said, "you must be sure that the Word of God is preached!"*

"Wherever there's a spiritual move," he said, "you must be *sure* that the Word of God is preached!"

This was one of many important lessons I would learn from him over the years of our involvement.

David Schoch - and Pastor Reg Layzell, who we would also get to know on our trip - were two sincere men of God who came out of the "latter rain" movement dedicated to protecting and keeping pure the fruit of that outpouring. While others twisted, distorted, and indulged in various chicanery, these men among a handful of others, preserved the essence of the Holy Spirit's great gifting.

I remember, also, when we walked into Pastor Layzell's church of Glad Tidings in Vancouver, British Columbia we experienced the same wonderful presence of the Lord we had encountered in Long Beach. Again, it moved me very deeply.

Pastor Layzell's church was different from Pastor Schoch's, at least architecturally. It was a brand new modern facility which seated eight hundred. However, like Pastor Schoch's church, it was packed.

Pastor Reg Layzell himself was as different in personality from David Schoch as the moon is from the sun. In the beginning he would scarcely pay me any attention. He'd once had a bad experience in Portland, and it was almost as if he held it against me. He was a stiff, proper Englishman of sixty, over six feet tall, gruff, straight to the point and dominating. Everyone was afraid of him, especially the children trying to skip Sunday school. He would track them down personally and return them to their classes. Nevertheless, the power of the Holy Spirit was on him in much the same way it was on David Schoch.

The result of that five week excursion - and especially the meetings with Pastors Schoch and Layzell - was to plant a passionate desire in me for the presence of the Lord. I committed myself at that time that I would do whatever it took to have God's presence in our church. That desire and that commitment have been the primary driving force in my life and ministry from that day to this. That was the turning point for me, my family and our congregation.

> *I committed myself at that time that I would do whatever it took to have God's presence in our church.*

In the spring of that same year, I told the church we were all going to go on a fast and that I was going to the coast to spend a week fasting and praying for direction for the future. While I was at the beach fasting and praying, the Lord spoke very clearly to me. He didn't say anything to me about the evangelistic field this time but instead gave me a charge to stay and shepherd His sheep.

Then He told me that He would do whatever I would believe Him for in the church. I felt almost as if He'd given me a blank check. I remembered the story of the prophet who told the king of Israel that he was to strike the ground with an arrow (2 Kings 13:15-19). When the king struck the ground three times and stopped the prophet rebuked him and told him that if he had struck the ground five or six times the Lord would have enabled him to defeat his enemies that many times. Believing that the Holy Spirit was saying He'd do in the church anything I could believe Him for, I made sure to ask largely. In fact, I decided to put down on paper everything I could possibly think of that a church should do. Afterwards, I went home and began to draw the layout of our church property on a blackboard, writing down on it everything I'd written at the beach. To this day, we refer to this experience simply as "the blackboard." Some of the things I wrote down were: *missionary work, Bible School, literature, branch churches, youth camp, old folks home, radio & television ministry.* Many of the things I wrote on that blackboard that day have wonderfully come to pass.

The Lord was beginning to give me a vision for our congregation, but it was still a frustrating time. I frankly had no doctrine of the church on which to base my new vision. I didn't really know what the church was all about. I still had to learn from the Scriptures what God was doing and why and where I fit into it as a pastor. Also, though I was beginning to preach on praise and the presence of the Lord, nothing was happening in the congregation. We still weren't growing.

During this time I began an intensive study of the Scriptures, looking for truth that would guide my ministry. The first area I began to search out was eschatology. A local pastor, John Kennington, began to give me a new theological perspective. John was a part of the Philadelphia Church movement and challenged me to reconsider my dispensationalism - whether it was Israel or the church that was the instrument of the Kingdom of God. I felt driven by the Lord to search the Scriptures. I thought I was studying to support dispensationalism, but the Lord had other ideas.

In fact, over the next two years I concluded that the church, specifically the local church, was God's instrument on Earth.   All my other views then began to change accordingly--my views of ministry, of evangelism, of local church government, as well as the role of the church in the present and in the future.   Convictions concerning the centrality of the local church, the unity of the Body, local church elders, and the triumph of the church, were planted in my heart and mind in those days and have continued to grow to the present day.

> *The church, specifically the local church, was God's instrument on Earth.*

The Lord was giving me new insight about the church, but I was still trying to produce it in my own efforts. I ran all the usual programs and some unusual ones. I even tried to have a Bible school - which lasted about two months. I also tried to finance the church myself, refusing for several years to take any salary.

In fact, my brothers and I were doing very well financially. As the family business prospered, my business successes contrasted strikingly with my lack of success with the church.

One morning I woke up and knew someone was in the room. At the foot of my bed I saw the dark form of a person. Then words began to come in my mind: "If you'll give youself to your business I will make you a millionare." I knew that if I said, "Yes," it would be a contract, a decision to move me out of the ministry and fully into business.

Then this demonic presence put the icing on the cake: "Then you can send missionaries all over the world," he said. I was greatly tempted by the offer. Suddenly I heard another voice - a quiet voice - saying "I don't need your money; I need you." It was clear what was at stake. The Lord was going to accomplish His will among us in His way and His time. All He wanted me to do was be yielded to Him.

During 1964, we began to have some of the new charismatic leaders visit Deliverance Temple. We

> *The Lord was going to accomplish His will among us in His way and His time.*

were never a traditional pentecostal church, for, I had negative feelings about the pentecostal-ism in which I had grown up. When the Lord began to pour out His spirit on the historical mainline denominational churches, though, we were very open to them. Gerald Derstine visited us in May, and soon other leaders were coming by to share with us as well.

Though I continued to invite Pastors Schoch and Layzell to Portland, it took almost three years before I could actually get them to come. In the meantime we tried everything to make the church grow. We tried "balloons and buses" and all the gimmicks and promotions we could think of, but nothing really seemed to work.

Around this time, I heard of another prophet by the name of Ernest Gentile, a friend of David Schoch and Reg Layzell. I asked Brother Gentile if he would be able to come to Portland and he agreed to do so. He ministered to the congregation for several nights in January of 1965.

At the end of the last service he turned to me on the platform and said, "Pastor, I have a word from the Lord for you." My heart leapt. I had heard of such a thing happening, but it had never happened to me. I was sure Brother Gentile was about to prophesy that the people ought to support me more, be more faithful, tithe faithfully - be better sheep.

I stood confidently before this man of God, in front of our congregation, as he began. These were the words he trumpeted for all to hear: "The evil that is in your heart is born of your own frustration! The problem is not the people, the problem is in you."

You can imagine the embarrassment I felt, knowing the people must have wondered what *kind* of evil was in my heart. At the same time I also felt good about the prophetic word. I knew there was a problem, but I had believed the problem was in the hearts of the people. I thought it was because I'd inherited a bad batch of sheep from my father and that we were incapable of going anywhere. Now the prophetic word had thrown a needed new light on the matter. My trouble was that I still could not pinpoint what the problem inside me was. One night soon afterward, as I was grumbling myself to sleep - my normal custom - and talking about this member and that, the Holy Spirit suddenly spoke very forcefully to me: "That is the evil in your heart. You are trying to shepherd a people you do not love, and that is evil in my sight."

I knew God had spoken to me and knew now

what the problem really had been. My heart was stricken before the Lord and I asked His forgiveness of this evil immediately. My repentance went so deep that I went before the church and told them what the Lord had spoken to me. I confessed that the evil in my heart was that I hadn't loved them as I needed to. I sincerely asked for their forgiveness, and for their prayers that the Lord would enable me in the future to love them as I should. I told them that if I stayed there the rest of my life, I would serve them and would do it with joy.

This, of course, was what the Lord was waiting for. From that moment on, things began to turn around in the church. Understanding of the body of Christ came to me, and I began to see the church as God saw it. I began to see the New Testament order and the importance of every member in the Body. My entire perspective was radically transformed. I now saw the church in a different light and realized I was to pastor this church. Since I knew God wanted me to stay home, I asked the Lord, since I couldn't go out, if He would somehow raise up ministry leaders under my ministry that would go over the wall.

S oon after my public repentance, Pastor Schoch agreed to come to Portland. I scheduled a "Deeper Life Crusade"for March 23-26, 1965. We scheduled a 10:00 a.m. service and 8:00 p.m. service; I set times of prayer and fasting and sent a letter to the members of the congregation concerning this special meeting.

৵৽

Pastor Schoch convinced Pastor Reg Layzell to meet him in Portland to spend a few days together. I was delighted to have two giants in the faith at our church at the same time. Furthermore, I was able to convince them to have a "double header" - meaning each of them would speak every night.

By this time our people were beginning to respond to the Holy Spirit and the Word in a new way and I think it was, because I'd changed. They were hungry for the moving of the Spirit and the presence of the Lord. God had promised us when we bought the theater back in 1959 that it would rain if we got the ark ready. Our hearts were filled with anticipation as we began the meetings.

I remember those precious times so well. Pastors Layzell and Schoch were so different individually and in their approaches to ministry, yet both brought with them the energizing power of the Holy Spirit. Brother Layzell emphasized the objective truth - the teaching of the Word which he did with great organization and thoroughness - while David Schoch's emphasis was more emotional, subjective truth - giving great words of prophecy (which nevertheless were grounded in the objective truth of the Word).

I especially remember the last service on Friday night when Reg Layzell spoke on his favorite subject, "the sacrifice of praise." I'd been teaching on praise and worship since my experience in 1962. Edie and I would stand on the platform and sing praises but we'd be by ourselves, as the congregation never joined in.

Brother Layzell spoke about the act of faith in worship. Because our background was divine healing and deliverance, faith and confession, we knew how to respond to God by faith. However, we had never connected it with praise and worship. That night the lights came on in the hearts of the people as they heard the message. They began to understand we are to offer our praise to the Lord whether we feel like it or not, simply because the Word of the Lord tells us to do so.

Reg Layzell spoke out of Hebrews 13:15, *"By Him therefore let us offer the sacrifice of praise to God continually, that is, the fruit of our lips giving thanks to his name."* He likened it to the Hebrew man in the Old Testament bringing his spotless lamb to be sacrificed on the Day of Atonement. He emphasized in his illustration that this was pedigree stock. This man had waited maybe years for a perfect lamb and now, instead of keeping it for breeding,

> *We are to offer our praise to the Lord whether we feel like it or not, simply because the Word of the Lord tells us to do so.*

he had to see it slaughtered and sacrificed to the Lord. Pastor Layzell asked the question, "How do you think the man felt giving up that spotless lamb?" The answer was that obviously he would have prefered not to. But, it was the Word of the Lord, so he offered the lamb and saw its throat slit, sacrificed before his eyes. It didn't matter whether he felt like doing it or not. He did it in obedience to the Word of the Lord. He did it as an act of faith.

Pastor Layzell said the sacrifice of praise was like that - a sacrifice not based on feelings or what had happened that week, but based on the Word of God. For over an hour he quoted scripture after scripture on how we were to offer up our praise to the Lord, - how we were to sing a new song, lifting our hands and worshiping as priests unto God, and how we needed to do so by faith based on God's Word.

I had spoken on praise and worship but never on it being an act of faith. You must remember our background was Pentecostal. We moved on feelings, not faith in the Word. If we felt good, we worshiped. Yet, at the same time, as a result of our background in the healing revival, we were a faith church. We knew about faith and how to respond in faith. So, as Pastor Layzell brought forth this word in a very clear and complete way, faith was released in our congregation.

After the message, I remember him doing something I thought very strange. He brought everybody forward to the front of the church. Then he stood at the altar and said, "Now we know it's God's Word to offer the sacrifice of praise so we're going to do it, as a sacrifice, by faith." He took his watch off his wrist and said, "For ten minutes we're going to offer the sacrifice of praise. I'll keep track of the time and you'll lift your hands, whether you feel like it or not, and for ten minutes sing praises to the Lord."

I thought this was a very mechanical approach and I felt uneasy about it. However, it was too late to do anything about it as the people were ready to do as Pastor Layzell had instructed.

We all stood there at the front of the church with our hands raised to the Lord. I remember Pastor Layzell beginning to sing loudly and not too melodically, "Hallelujah, praise your holy name, thank you Lord." And we all - by faith - followed him. We began to sing praises to the Lord, not because we felt like it, but because we had heard the Word of the Lord and were compelled to act on it by faith.

At first it was very awkward. I felt embarrassed

that we were worshiping God in such a mechanical way. However, within a minute or two we seemed to shift gears. I could hear a spiritual release beginning and, before long, a roar of praise rose up from our gathered congregation. The people moved into a dimension of worship that I'd experienced three years before in Long Beach and then again in Vancouver.

I watched tears stream down the faces of various individuals as we all stood for ten minutes and worshiped the Lord with abandon. For a moment I felt like we had gone to heaven. This was what I had wanted more than breath itself. I had wanted the presence of God manifested in the midst of our church, and now we were experiencing it. You could almost physically feel the holy presence of the Lord covering the people as He had truly come into our midst. From then on we were never the same again.

The volume of that praise lifted us as a congregation into a whole new dimension in the Kingdom of God. But all of a sudden, as we were lifting up the high praises of God, Pastor Layzell took the mic and stopped us. "All right, time's up. Stop now." he said. You can't imagine the frustration I felt. For the first time our church was experiencing true worship, and now he was stopping it--because the time was up! That was Pastor Layzell though, forever a man of his word and regardless of the fact that we were at a turning point in the life of our congregation. He'd said we were to worship for ten minutes and that's exactly how long he gave us. In analyzing what came about, it's important to note again that there are two kinds of truth: objective and subjective. We need both kinds in balance. In my early life and ministry everything was based on subjective truth - and we never grew. We had a lot of good feelings - subjective (emotional) truth - but no real fruit. Then objective truth - God's Word - came to us concerning the sacrifice of praise, objective truth about a subjective experience. And we have never been the same since.

If we build on a subjective truth we will have a temporary experience at best. If we build with objective truth and allow our subjective experiences to be defined and guided by it, then we'll be able to build for the long term and bear fruit that remains. Pastor Layzell had laid a foundation of objective truth concerning praise and worship and the presence of the Lord, and now we were experiencing it in a wonderful way.

> *If we build with objective truth and allow our subjective experiences to be defined and guided by it then we'll be able to build for the long term and bear fruit that remains.*

Our two guests could not stay with us over the weekend. We were a very small church and I was afraid we wouldn't be able to give them an appropriate honorarium. I wrote a check for $250 to each of the men, thinking it was probably not enough. I sealed the envelopes and handed them to the two in my office, assuming they wouldn't be opened until later. Brother Layzell, however, proceeded to take out his glasses and to open his envelope on the spot. He pulled out the check, looked at it and then threw it down on my desk - leaving little doubt he was offended at our small honorarium.

However, to my relief he said, "Nobody's worth that kind of money!" He wasn't offended! I picked up the check and said, "Brother Layzell, couldn't you use it for missions?" I knew he had a great missionary church in Vancouver, B.C. Immediately he grabbed it back out of my hand and said, "Well, that's different."

All my past heros, both when I was a teen and when I was a healing evangelist, had fallen, but after 1965, Pastor Reg Layzell became a spiritual father to me.   He deposited three truths that became foundational for us: unity, prayer, and worship.   He also encouraged us to have a set prayer room - to have pre-service prayer - which we do to this day.   "What brings revival," he'd say, "maintains revival." (meaning prayer).   We owe him an eternal debt of gratitude.

Our next service after the conclusion of the meetings was Sunday morning, and it was going to be without David Schoch and Reg Layzell. This was the test! If God had really deposited something in us, we were going to find out that Sunday.

To begin with, as a result of the midweek meetings, we were short six hundred dollars. In those days that was a lot of money and we needed a good offering to cover the short-fall.

I remember that as we started the service that

Sunday morning we immediately moved into our worship time and the presence of the Lord was still with us in the same way we had experienced it a few nights earlier. I was so thrilled! Most of the time when we had meetings the personality of the evangelist was what fueled whatever happened. When he went, the revival went with him. For the first time a deposit had been left behind, and the same presence of the Lord was with us.

I told the congregation at the beginning of worship that we needed financial help and told them that we were just going to lift our hands and worship the Lord and afterwards give as a sacrifice of praise as well. As we began to worship the Lord, one by one the members came forward with their offerings.

That day God proved something to me that has been with me all the rest of my ministry. When you are in the will of God, the finances will always be there. The exact amount of money we needed came in that Sunday. Not only that, but immediately afterward, without any increase in the number of people, the offerings doubled every month. We had been lifted up to a new level of giving as well as worshiping. After all, giving, if rightly understood, is worship. Both are offerings which we sacrifice to the Lord.

> *That day God proved something to me that has been with me all the rest of my ministry. When you are in the will of God, the finances will always be there.*

The revival with Pastors Schoch and Layzell was one of the most important "set times," in my life and in the life of our congregation. Everything we are doing today has its roots in that visitation.

Whenever a congregation truly worships God in spirit and truth, and unity, the presence of the Lord comes in a special way. The anointing of the Lord comes upon the church and its leaders, and, for me, the Word of God was opened up in a new way. My eyes were opened, and everywhere I looked in the Bible I saw the glorious church.

CHAPTER 11

I t was a time of the old passing away and a time of renewal, yet, always remained threads of connection. It was a time when my dad passed on to be with the Lord, followed soon after by the birth of our fourth daughter, Tracey. It was a time when Brother George Evans visited our church and, during his altar call, my 80 year old grandmother and my eight year old daughter Diane while standing side by side, were gloriously baptized in the Holy Spirit.

∾∾

During the last years of his life, my dad and I were in great harmony and my only regret is that he didn't live long enough to see the effects of the great breakthrough in our congregation. The day before he died - and I had no idea he was going to die - I visited him in the hospital. It was strange because I did something I'd never done before. I shaved him, and, looking back on it, it was as though it had fallen to me to prepare him for his journey.

That night I dreamt about him and he came to me smiling and saying, "I'm going home." He said it three times and in my mind and in the dream I thought he just meant he was going to the house.

In the morning, though, I got a phone call that he'd gone on to be with Jesus. I've always believed the dream was the Lord's way of letting me know that my dear old daddy was all right.

I should say a little more here about my beautiful daughter Tracey. Before she was born, we had already been blessed with three great daughters, Debi, Diane and Brenda, and everyone was sure Tracey would be a boy. Some even prophesied it, but the Lord had other ideas. On the first Sunday morning after her birth, I stood in front of the congregation with a paper bag in my hand.

"I have a lot of these to sell," I joked, pulling out a pair of bib overalls while, nevertheless, feeling a great joy for Tracey's safe arrival.

Sometime after Dad's death, the Lord began dealing with me about the name of our church, *Deliverance Temple*. As I was sitting at my desk one day, I received a call from the telephone company wanting to sell us advertising space in the yellow pages. The girl on the line mentioned that over ten thousand phone numbers had been changed in our prefix. This meant ten thousand new families had moved into our area, many of whom were probably looking for a church. I thought to myself, what would *Deliverance Temple* mean to those ten thousand people. Supposing they were just nominal Christians and wanted their children to go to Sunday School some place, if they saw a building that said "Set Free Temple," what would it communicate to them? Would they be apt to send their children over to our Sunday School? I doubted it. They probably thought their children were plenty free enough and I really believed the word "Deliverance", in a changing time and outside our immediate church circle, would be interpreted in that way.

Then the Lord revealed a principle that has been very important to me ever since. He told me, "Son, you can't build a church on an emphasis or you won't grow." Deliverance was our emphasis.

We didn't have a bad name in the city. My mom and dad were good honest people, and I really didn't want to get rid of my father's memory and the name he'd given the church. So I talked to my mother about what the Lord was showing me. I explained that we were building on a new emphasis and that our name didn't really reflect what God was now doing. She immediately agreed that the name should be changed.

Thus, we began to call ourselves "Bible Deliverance Temple" for a season, putting "Deliverance" in small letters so Bible Temple would stand out. Soon afterwards, we dropped "Deliverance" and became "Bible Temple."

As the church began to move in the new supernatural dimension, the spiritual life of the church was greatly and quickly heightened. I noticed it first among the young people. We still

The church began to move in the new supernatural dimension . . .

had less than a hundred and fifty people in the congregation, and, in fact, almost half of those were young - in part I think because I was still only thirty-five years old and looked more like a youth pastor than a senior pastor.

I remember one Sunday morning when a petition was handed to me by Wayman Steele, a teenager who attended the church, signed by forty-two teenagers requesting that the first three rows in the church be reserved for them. While I was used to having them sit in the last three rows, obviously I was glad to grant them their request - establishing a tradition which has remained with us to the present day.

Also, after fifteen years of existence as a church without one single young person ever wanting to go into the ministry, suddenly, a dozen young people came forward to declare that they felt called. After agreeing with them in prayer, we sent them off to a number of traditional Bible colleges.

When the school year was finished, they came home for the summer and asked to see me. I remember meeting with them and listening to their request that, instead of sending them away, I train them for the ministry myself.

It was quite a challenge, to say the least. I had no formal ministerial training myself, and wondered how I could possibly give these young people formal training. Yet I knew they were speaking the truth - that I shouldn't send them away. They wanted, besides studying the Bible, to drink of the river of God that was flowing so strongly now in their own local church. We needed to find a way for them to do both.

As I began to pray about it, my eyes were opened to see that, during that time of refreshing, God had brought into our body some very capable teachers, men who had formal training and also identified with the vision the Lord had given us. Bob Stricker had been trained in the United Brethren Church and, had become a pastor there, and Dr. David Blomgren had graduated from Portland's Western Conservative Baptist Seminary.

We sat down together and began to discuss the possibility of starting our own Bible college with David Blomgren taking the lead. At that time, the United States was entering into the Vietnam War. In order for our young people to be able to stay in Bible college, we needed to structure the school program in a very specific and complete way. We had to have teachers, curriculum, a library, a full time schedule, classrooms, dorms, and so on. Only in that way would our students be given the exemptions they needed to stay and study for the ministry - a fact the Lord used in leading us to do it the right way from the beginning.

The church was now approaching three hundred members and was growing every year. Still, we were a very small congregation to be launching a full time Bible college and many people thought it just wouldn't be possible, with our limited resources - both financial and otherwise. However, in the fall of 1967, Portland Bible College was birthed with

> *We didn't know we couldn't start a Bible college. So we did!*

sixteen full-time students. God started a work that has since launched scores of pastors throughout the lives of thousands.

It is said that the bumble bee can't fly. It is aerodynamically impossible. His body is too heavy for his wings. However, no one has ever informed the bumble bee. We didn't know we couldn't start a Bible college. So we did!

I was President, David Blomgren the Vice President, and Bob Stricker the Dean of Students. Ben Taylor and Nelson Miller were also members of our initial faculty. We all sacrificed many hours to do the necessary teaching. That first year we had sixteen full-time and seven part-time students. Of the full-timers, seven came from outside of Bible Temple. From the beginning, the Lord used PBC to train leaders for many other local churches besides Bible Temple.

We developed our courses from scratch and wrote our own notes. Eventually, we bound those notes together and published them as books: *Present Day Truths*, *The Holy Spirit Today*, *Local Church*, and others. In 1965, I'd purchased our first printing press and became - without any training - our first pressman. In this way, Portland Bible College gave birth to Bible Temple Publications, which now annually distributes tens of thousands of books around the world.

As it was impossible to find charismatic books in

the local Christian bookstores, we also opened a bookstore, purchasing a building across the street from the church to house it along with the printing press. Thus, the portion of the original "blackboard" vision that had to do with *literature* was fulfilled.

Throughout the late 1960's the Lord continued to bless Bible Temple. The church continued to grow, and the college also grew. God sent in young people from all over the country, as well as from our own area; so, of course, more teachers came as well. Houses became available in the area, and we bought them to use as dormitories. Little by little, we bought up most of the land around the church. The second year of PBC saw a two hundred and fifty-two percent increase in enrollment with outside students from six states and two foreign countries. Time and time again God marvelously provided facilities for all we had to do.

> *Throughout the late 1960's the Lord continued to bless Bible Temple. The church continued to grow, and the college also grew.*

Kevin Conner visited from Australia for the first time during our August Family Camp in 1969 and came on a regular basis after that. Kevin is an excellent Bible teacher who shared in the vision the Lord had given me. Eventually, Kevin moved his family to Bible Temple and joined our staff as a full time teacher and finally as the Dean of Portland Bible College. He returned to his native Australia in 1980, but he left a permanent deposit in our church.

Also in the realm of education, our tape ministry was begun in 1970 and has opened up more nations to us than anything else we've ever done. Edie was recovering from surgery at home and asked that we buy a tape recorder and record the service. Then Errol Livesay, a longstanding member of the church, caught the vision to "rehear the word" and started taping the services with six separate tape recorders at once. After that, we purchased duplicating equipment and within two years, began sending out twenty thousand tapes a year all over the world. Our tapes were unique and had a special power, because, in addition to a message from the Word on one side, we included excerpts from the worship service on the other. The inclusion of worship has set our tape ministry apart and accounts for the tremendous world wide demand.

People write in and say "We enjoy your messages, but oh the worship!" This is as it should be, because praising and worshiping the Lord is key in our house. When it's strong, everything else is right. Our hearts are opened to the Word and the prophetic ministry can flow. It's also true that the tapes - along with our books - have reached far more people than I ever would have as a traveling evangelist.

Eventually, the Lord gave us a vision for starting a kindergarten through twelfth grade school and we began to pray about purchasing the overhead garage door company building that was next to us. The property was commercially zoned making it possible to be used for an educational facility. I remember a time when we even laid hands on the building, asking God to remove the owners so we could build. We felt in some way the Lord would curse them so they would have to leave.

God didn't curse them. Instead, He blessed them and greatly increased their business to the point that, it wasn't long before they came to us, saying their business was doing so well, they needed to move. They asked if we would be interested in buying their building and by 1974 we had begun our re-modeling for the school.

Because we were going to start as an A.C.E. school, I, as pastor, was required to be the school's principal for the first year. This meant I had to submit myself for training.

I've always felt inferior when it comes to academic things. My dad only went through the eighth grade and didn't encourage me to apply myself. I never got good grades. Therefore, I called the A.C.E. headquarters and told them I wanted to send Larry Wade, the man who really would be administrating the school, to get the training. In fact, Larry had been the one who had done all the research and all the preparation for starting the school.

The response was, "Well, Pastor, it sounds like you're really too busy to have a school."

I said "No, we really want to have a school."

"OK, then as the Pastor you are going to have to come down and get the training." They wouldn't let me off the hook.

I booked a "red eye" special and flew overnight

to Dallas. I checked into a motel around 6:00 a.m. and went on to the training center at 8:00 a.m. As if being the only charismatic there wasn't bad enough, I struggled with an inferiority complex as a relatively uneducated man in the midst of educators.

I sat at a desk and went through the first "P.A.C.E." and came to the first pre-test only to discover that I couldn't remember ever having read anything that sounded like what they were asking. I began to get very nervous.

In fact, it took me the whole morning to finally pass that first pre-test while, in the meantime, all the other trainees had gone through at least one or two entire P.A.C.E.'s I was so uptight I could hardly think at all. I was perspiring profusely and the odor was beginning to distract me. By about two in the afternoon while I was still on my first P.A.C.E., a thought kept badgering me, "Just run! Get out now!" After all I had another eleven P.A.C.E.'s to complete in order to finish the program. It was beginning to look like I would flunk out.

One of the supervisors must have noticed my frustration so he came over to me and said, "I think you're ready to be tested on number one." I went up to the testing table with my mind completely blank. That same supervisor must have seen the blank look on my face, too, because he fudged - he came over and said, "Well, what about this . . ." and led me through the test.

By this time, I was absolutely convinced that I was too dumb to pass through the training and as a result, we'd never have our school. At the end of the day I went back to my motel room, fell across the bed and prayed, "God, I can't do this. If you don't help me we'll never have a school." Then I fell asleep with all my clothes on.

When I woke up the next morning, my mind was sharper than I'd ever known it to be. It was absolutely miraculous. I went into the learning center and ran through the P.A.C.E.'s with complete ease. In fact, I was the second one to finish the entire training course - and with good grades. I knew then that the Lord definitely wanted us to have a school.

T he Jesus Movement hit the West Coast
in the early 1970's, and many of the
"Jesus People" came to Bible Temple
and Portland Bible College. We seemed to
draw young people who'd been converted
already, and who'd concluded they needed
more discipline added to their lives. Though
we didn't have the great "hippy harvest" of
some places, we did reap a harvest of many
excellent young people.

ॐॐ

Some of these "Jesus People" are now great
leaders in the Body of Christ who have been sent
out from us. Others remained and are now among
our elders. Young men like Frank Damazio, Ken
Malmin, Mike Herron, Wendell Smith, Bill Scheidler,
Jan Weinstein, Jack Louman, Rick Johnston and
Ken Wilde came to the school as students and
eventually became leaders in Bible Temple and

around the world.

In the beginning of 1972, the Lord began dealing with me about eldership and the concept of team ministry. At that time, in addition to the added responsibilities engendered by the Bible college, the printing press and the tape ministry, we had grown to be a church of eight hundred people. I, however, continued to function as if we had remained at a hundred. If people wanted prayer or counsel or help of any sort, they came directly to me. There was no place else to go. I was the pastor, I ran the show.

The problem wasn't that I didn't have good men around me. I even had men designated as elders. However, they weren't being honored as elders or used as elders either.

I've often likened the experience to running a crisis center, where finally the only people I had time to talk with were those in the most serious trouble - those who were dying or getting a divorce or grieving for children who had run away. Another image that came to mind was of Edie and me standing at the bottom of a cliff and running to catch people as they fell off. Yet we never had enough time to go up on top and build a proper fence to keep others from falling.

The Lord spoke to me at this time and asked if I wanted to pastor a crowd or a family. Of course, His question went straight to the heart of it. I was too conscientious ever to want to pastor a crowd - to be a "pulpiteer," who gave a Sunday message and went home. I genuinely cared for people and wanted to know about them. I was trying my very best to pastor the eight hundred that God had entrusted into my care. However, it was getting to the point that when I met "new people" in the congregation, I was afraid to ask how long they'd been coming for fear they'd say "three years." I knew it was a losing battle. In addition to this pastoral difficulty, I was starting to have chest pains which the doctor warned me were the first signs of what had killed my dad.

What was needed was a pastoral team - trained elders to act as "district pastors" and minister to the needs of our people who were scattered throughout different areas of the city. The blueprint for it was quite clear in the Scriptures and, using the Word as our guide, we soon restructured our church government accordingly.

> *I was afraid to ask how long they'd been coming for fear they'd say "three years." I knew it was a losing battle.*

Before we'd essentially governed the church through a trustee board, made up of myself and several deacons. But, we found scripture was clear. Church government was never to be in the hands of deacons but rather was to be administered by those men called to one of the five fold ministries of apostle, pastor, evangelist, prophet or teacher. These elders in turn could appoint deacons, could enlist the help of businessmen, etcetera but they themselves needed to be called. Thus, what we instituted was not a democracy, but neither was it a one man show. It was an eldership and it came directly from God's Word.

During the fall of 1973, I ordained the elders and had them begin home meetings in addition to our regular services. We divided the area into ten "districts," each led by a district elder. Our original elders were: Dean Bennett, Kevin Conner, Ivan Correll, Robin Johnson, Leo Kaylor, Bob Stricker, Jack Talbott, Ben Taylor, Ira Washburn and Larry Wade.

It was a reorganization that no doubt saved my life, and at the same time, benefitted the congregation enormously. Needs were met; people were more in touch with their leadership; and the burden for crisis management was lifted from Edie and me and shared among the others. I believe that this concept is a key with large churches. Pastors in general tend to believe they can do all things better and so must do all things. After a while, that attitude becomes counter productive. Ultimately, one person can do only so much and there are only so many hours in the day. Furthermore, I believe members (elders) are much happier when they are genuinely participating and contributing.

I should say here that, in case I made it sound like I was all alone before really activating the eldership, I was not doing justice to the remarkable family with which our Lord so blessed me. From the earliest days of our church, Edie stood by my side with unwavering faithfulness, serving in very important and highly visible ministries - as worship leader, head of our Sunday school, Dean of Women Students at PBC and in leadership of the Women's Ministries. In addition, she assisted in so many of the aforementioned "rescue missions". But, by far her most important contribution came by her daily practice of speaking faith into my life.

We have been through some dark days together but I don't ever remember Edie saying - even in the darkest of those hours - "Will God come through?" or, "Will we make it? What do you think is going to happen to us?" Even when I walked the floors, wrestling with my own doubts and fears, she always spoke faith. I never would have made it without her.

In addition, there were my daughters - Debra, Diane, Brenda, and Tracey - who always thought of Bible Temple as "our church," not "Dad's church" and who gave of themselves accordingly. It was such a blessing over the years to see them contribute as "Edie's team" in the Sunday school and later on watch them take up other positions of increased responsibility.

Debra, who has a degree in teaching, teaches in our grade school to this day and has written curriculum for pre-schoolers, besides teaching for 25 years in our children's program. Diane was my secretary for eight years before getting married and later served with her husband as children's pastors. Brenda also taught in the school before starting her family, and, Tracey was the church receptionist before taking over the leadership of the nursery.

In fact, my daughters have labored on staff or as volunteers in almost every department of the church at one time or another. They have been the joy of my life. Raising them in the house of God has been an absolute delight, as they've always responded positively. They have not caused hurt or disappointment, and their commitment to Jesus Christ as children brought them through all of their turbulent teenage days unbroken by sin.

Outside of the Lord Jesus Himself, I can truthfully say, the next most important source of strength and support in my life has been my four daughters and their mother.

While on the subject of eldership and team ministry, I need to mention a derivative that bore fruit later on, though not without considerable pain. In the late 1970's my friend, Pastor Dick Benjamin, visited us from Abbott Loop Christian Center in Anchorage, Alaska and gave us a specific vision for church planting - a vision for sending out teams of people and not just individual church planters.

Thus, the process of church planting and the sending of missionaries was greatly accelerated during the first part of the 1980's. During a two year period of time, many of our most prominent leaders formed church planting teams and were sent out. These were men who had played a prominent role in the decade of the 1970's - intricately involved in the life and ministry of Bible Temple. Our music leader, the dean of the Bible college, the head of our counselling ministry, the principal of our high school, several teachers from the Bible college, and several district pastors, all left in the early 1980's. In one year alone, nine elders and their wives went out from us to pioneer churches from the west coast to the east coast, and even overseas.

While on the one hand we were excited to see the increase take place for the sake of the Kingdom, on the other hand our hearts were bleeding with the constant saying of goodbyes to our friends. We knew they would go out and succeed in fulfilling the call of God, but we also knew they would never return. It seemed to be at our expense and at times the price seemed to be too high. In fact, some of the members even got a vision for going out to another *local* church in our area. At that we drew the line. So many legitimate teams going out apparently shook some others loose as well.

I can remember Sunday after Sunday saying goodbye to team after team, with the other elders gathered around and with people weeping and showing their love. I didn't always like it, yet I knew that as the congregation rose in obedience being called for by the Lord, the work of God would go forward.

One of the things I learned that year was that it pays to train as many potential leaders in a congregation as possible. It's not enough to have "staff" leaders. It's also vitally important to have a continual stream of lay leaders flowing into places of responsibility. In athletics, if you're going to have a championship team, you can't have a strong first string only, your second string has to be strong as well. It's the same with growing successful churches.

Many skeptics came to me in those days and said the glory days at Bible Temple were coming to an end. We were losing all of our great dynamic leaders, and things would never be the same. However, in my spirit, I knew that wasn't true. I can honestly say that those who stepped into the vacant leadership slots did as good if not a better job than those who had gone out from us. As confirmation, the church continued to prosper and grow.

Charles Green, the pastor of Word of Faith Temple in New Orleans, was our special Family Camp speaker in August of 1971. The place was full during those meetings, packed to the doors. One night as Brother Green stood to speak he gave a very strong prophetic word: "The place is too straight and too tight! Rise up and build, for I will make you a praise in this city!"

The word of the Lord came to us and we knew it was true. We were to rise and build. However, we were land locked. We thought we had bought all the land we could in our neighborhood, so we immediately believed it meant relocation outside the city limits.

The next Sunday the place was full to capacity again. As I was speaking, a visitor came in. I watched him as he walked down the aisle, a young man in his early twenties, casually dressed. The ushers had missed him and he was looking for an empty seat. I followed him as he looked down row after row without success. As I continued to speak he came all the way down to the front. Finally, I stopped preaching and just watched, feeling really sorry for him. By now he was standing in the front of the whole church, and still no usher came to help him. All was silent and every eye was on him.

I remember his turning to the congregation and stating, "There's no room in this place. It's too tight!" In response to which, everybody broke out laughing. I'm sure he thought we were very rude but that's what the prophet had just told us. Of course, then someone helped him find a seat but he had unknowingly confirmed the word of the Lord. Afterward, I began to look for property outside of town so we could relocate. I looked at scores of parcels out in the countryside but, for one reason or another, all to no avail. Either the property wasn't what we needed or in several instances, when we actually made offers, sales were never consummated. My diligent efforts to fulfill the prophetic word were causing much frustration.

Then a most amazing thing took place. David Schoch came to Bible Temple for our "prophetic assembly" in April, 1973, and one morning when he began to prophesy, his word was almost a rebuke to us. "Rise up and don't profane my word. Knock out these four walls and build as I said." Then he prophesied that we should go back and listen to what the Lord had already said to us.

Even as he spoke I thought to myself, "There's no way we can knock out these four walls." We had attempted to buy the remaining land behind us and to the side of us but it was not available. Now the Lord was saying to rise up and knock out the four walls.

Brother Schoch continued, "Even now the walls are falling." I thought to myself, "I sure hope you are in the Spirit, Brother Schoch, because there's no way we can build any more here." Also, I worried that what he'd said would bring confusion to the people who had supported my efforts to buy out in the suburbs.

The very same day of the prophecy, one of the Bible college students came to me and said, "You know, the home that joins our property in the back of the building?" I said "Yes," knowing it quite well as that particular piece of property was critical if we were ever to build more in that neighborhood. The house was on a very large lot and I'd tried to buy it many times. However, since the owners hated the church, they had absolutely refused to sell.

"Well," the student went on, "last night something strange happened. We heard this loud crash like a car wreck and when we went outside to investigate, we discovered that the retaining wall on that property had fallen down."

The full length of that retaining wall which had stood in front of the house for probably fifty or sixty years had fallen over onto the sidewalk for no apparent reason. Suddenly I remembered the prophecy, "even now the walls are falling." And, of course, the prophet had spoken with no knowledge of what was going on outside.

I went back into the office and asked our administrator, Warren Steele, to write a check for ten thousand dollars. He looked at me with amazement and said we didn't have ten thousand in the bank. I told him to write the check anyway and I would make sure it was covered. I knew the Holy Spirit had spoken to us and that God was doing something supernatural.

I walked over to the neighbor's house and knocked on the door. I'd talked to him many times in the past, and he'd always mocked the church while refusing to sell. This time, though, when he came to the door and I asked him again he agreed to sell. Of course, he wanted more than it was worth - fifty thousand - but I gave him the ten thousand dollar check as earnest money and within thirty days we'd raised the additional forty thousand from among the congregation. The wall falling down as confirmation of the prophetic word was a rather dramatic testimony as to what the Lord wanted us to do.

Brother Schoch had also prophesied that we were to go back and listen to what God had previously said, and, when we did go back to Charles Green's prophetic word we found it very interesting. The word of the Lord that came through Brother Green was that we were to rise and build for the Lord was going to make us a praise *in the city.* We then realized our searching for acreage outside the city limits had not been intended by the Lord. We were to be a praise in the city! So we committed ourselves to building where we were.

We immediately launched a fund raising project and began to buy up other properties in the general area, both for parking and for the Bible college. We also began to draw up plans for a new auditorium to seat fifteen hundred people.

ABOVE: Our famous "blackboard" - 1962. BELOW LEFT: Deliverance Temple, 1957 - Old Granada Theater. BELOW RIGHT: Inside the theater.

LEFT: Bible Temple Family - 1973. **BELOW:** Bible Temple - 1973.

✧⁓✧

LEFT: Glisan St Property.

BELOW: New sanctuary at Glisan Street - Dedicated 1979

BELOW: Our last Sunday at our Glisan Street facility - October 1991.

✧⁓✧

ABOVE: Bible Temple Community Center - 1995. **BELOW:** First service in our new building on Rocky Butte - October 1991.

RIGHT: 1966. **BELOW:** 1969.

BOTTOM: The Iverson Family - 1973.

ABOVE: My brothers Morrie and Neil
(Tom Dick & Harry). **RIGHT:** 1962.
BOTTOM: 1975.

LEFT: 1984. **BELOW:** Mark & Diane Bryan, Todd & Tracey Ebeling, Dick & Edie Iverson, Phil & Debi Zedwick, Mark & Brenda Sligar.

LEFT: Debra, Diane, Brenda, Tracey - 1995.

The Iverson
Family -
1994

I t may sound from here on that our experience as a church has centered around building facilities. However, that's not the case. Though indisputably there has been a lot of building, we have never built just for the sake of building. We've had to build simply because of the steady growth we've experienced.

     ❦

Ever since God visited us in 1965, we have grown steadily averaging nearly ten percent growth per year for thirty years. Our facilities have filled up; we've gone to double services, and they've filled up again. Finally we've been forced to expand. Buildings for us have served as places to preserve the harvest the Lord keeps giving us.

However, God has used natural things to teach us spiritual truths. He has used the necessity of constructing buildings and the faith required to do so to ingrain into our people the spirit of perseverance, the spirit of sacrifice, and the spirit of faith.   He has enlarged us spiritually as well as naturally, and we are better for it.

In December of 1973, we submitted our preliminary building plans to the city for our new auditorium and an L-shaped educational facility to be located behind the theater. We had a very capable

> *God has used natural things to teach us spiritual truths.*

in-house architect in Ira Washburn; we had a heart to work, and I thought it was going to be simple. Little did I know what lay ahead.

When I went to the planning commission to get permission to build, I found out that first we had to go to the neighborhood association before going to the planning commission.   I was unaware that there was a neighborhood association in our area. Despite my ignorance, the neighbors were very offended that we hadn't gone to them before going to City Hall.   By the time we were able to meet with them, in fact, a movement to oppose our request had already gathered a full head of steam.

We met in the auditorium of the area grade school in January of 1974. Never had I been the recipiant of so much hatred as I was that night. We were accused of destroying their community. We were told we should get out of town. We were attacked for bringing in a lot of "undesirable young people" from out of state.   Ultimately, the recommendation to the planning commission was that we not be allowed to build and expand further.

We knew we had received the word of the Lord that we were to arise and knock out our four walls, so it was the word of the Lord against the word of the neighborhood association. However, it seemed that all of our attempts to appease were to no avail.

When we went to our meeting with the planning commission, once again the influence of the neighborhood and opposition in the heavenlies were against us. The level of hate was even stronger at this second meeting. After a number of hearings, on July 2, 1974, we received the planning commission's negative ruling. The official recommendation to City Hall was that our permit be denied, and one of the ten stated reasons for the rejection was that there were too many churches in the area already.

We were stunned by the city's decision. We thought we were doing a good job for the neighborhood and city. We especially couldn't understand why there would be objections to our having godly young people in the neighborhood. With the word of the Lord to draw from, we appealed the decision.

The meeting to consider our appeal was with the mayor and the city council. It was another open hearing where neighbors could come and express themselves. The planning commission, of course, would recommend to the mayor and city council that we be turned down. With everyone and everything against us, the situation would have seemed hopeless - but for the word of the

Lord.

Desiring wisdom from the Holy Spirit, I went away to a motel to fast for three days bringing with me all the commission's reasons for denial. I didn't believe that I should hire an attorney to answer those questions for us. As the pastor, I wanted to answer the questions the way the Lord would answer them. The Lord was faithful to help me during those days of seeking Him, as I put together a written presentation with pictures and maps, answering each of the ten objections raised.

By this time the local media had picked up the controversy between Bible Temple and the neighborhood association. When we arrived at City Hall, the television cameras and various news reporters were there to cover the event.

> The Lord was faithful to help me during those days of seeking Him

Inside the council chambers, the mayor sat up front, flanked on either side by the various city councilmen. Feeling somewhat intimidated, I approached the podium to present our case. I began by reading through our answers to each of the ten objections of the Planning Commission. I then responded to each one. The first objection, the erosion of the quality of the residential neighborhood; the second, the conversion of single family housing units for use by the Bible college. As I moved on to the third, the resulting reduced livability of the neighboring residential units, I noticed the mayor was reading ahead. I'm sure he was taking note of all the inequities on which the denial had been based.   The denial was clearly prejudicial, illegal and unconstitutional, and I think our answers confirmed that beyond a doubt.

Before I could address the fourth objection, that there were already too many religious facilities in our neighborhood, the mayor stopped me. He said he'd decided to negotiate personally between the neighborhood's complaints and the church's needs. He refused to let me read further and brought the hearing to a close.

I knew the mayor had to have concluded that the denial was illegal, and that he would have to find another way to stop us. Out of respect for his office we had to accept his offer to negotiate.

We began what was a strange series of events. I met alone with the mayor after he'd already met with the neighborhood association and the planning commission. He immediately let me know that he didn't want any more large churches built in the city of Portland. He also stated emphatically that he didn't want any more "black top jungle" church parking lots in his city either.   From that inauspicious starting point, the negotiations proceeded.

> *"Man will try to put boundaries on my house and no more than they can put boundaries to the sand of the sea and change God's boundary at the ocean, than they can limit the house of God."*

During that time we were strengthened again by a word from the Lord, which came to us through

Brother Ernest Gentile's prophecy: "Man will try to put boundaries on my house and no more than they can put boundaries to the sand of the sea and change God's boundary at the ocean, neither can they limit the house of God." While we were trying to cooperate with the neighborhood association and to address their legitimate complaints, we first and foremost needed to remain faithful to our God.

Finally we came to the climactic night of January 3, 1975. I'll never forget it. We all met in one of the city's buildings. The representatives of Bible Temple met with the mayor in one room while in turn the neighborhood association met with him just down the hall. The mayor would come to us and discuss our concerns and then go to discuss the concerns of the neighborhood association - or so we thought.

After we'd negotiated for several hours the mayor came to us and said, "Look, Pastor, these people are fanatics and radicals, and they'll do anything to stop you from building. You're just going to have to give more." We agreed to compromise, and he began to limit the size of the building, the school, and anything on which we seemed willing to negotiate. He seemed to be so concerned that we ultimately have the opportunity to build, that I sincerely tried to work with him. He gave me every impression that he was really with us and so I did everything I could to bend and compromise. This went on until 2:00 a.m.

Finally, he said there was just one more thing the neighborhood association wanted from us. Something told me I shouldn't have compromised as much as I had already, but I thought giving in on one last minor point probably wouldn't hurt our plans all that much. I agreed to it.

The mayor walked out of the room, saying he thought we were finally ready for a written agreement on the limitations we'd discussed - one of which was that we'd agree to return all the single family dwellings to their former use; and another stipulating that we could never buy another piece of property in the city without prior city approval. I doubted that the latter would ever stand up in court, but in the name of cooperation I agreed to it anyway.

I became more and more uneasy, though, and was increasingly convinced I was giving in more than I should.

The mayor walked out of our room at 2:00 a.m. and said he would go down the hall and make sure the neighborhood representatives were ready to sign the document. Being thirsty, I left our group soon afterward and went down the hall to the drinking fountain. As it turned out, the fountain was right next to where the neighborhood association and the mayor were meeting. I didn't go down there purposely to eavesdrop. Nevertheless, the door was open and I could hear.

"We've got to squeeze these people more until they agree to get out of town," I heard the mayor say. "So let's come up with some more objections that will force them to give up and not build."

At first I couldn't believe what I was hearing. I'd thought the mayor was on our side - not on the side of those "fanatics and radicals," as he called them. I'd been duped and taken in, falling for all of his proposed compromises, which were really designed to keep us from building in the city. I was stunned and irate!

I walked back down that hall to where our brethren were waiting for me, and as I walked, I remembered the prophetic word: "They will try to put boundaries on you, but they will not be able to do so - they cannot limit God." I felt like I'd betrayed the Lord in accepting all the compromises and I prayed, "Lord, please forgive me and give me an opportunity to get out of these negotiations."

In a few minutes, the mayor walked in and said that there was only one more thing the neighborhood association wanted from us. I had my way out.

I stood up and said "Mister Mayor, I'm sorry but this negotiation is over. We're not going to agree to any of the things that have been discussed this evening. We're withdrawing from these negotiations." At this point the mayor became enraged. "You can't do this!" he shouted. "I've worked all night to get an agreement out of the neighborhood association. You can't walk out now!"

"Well, we are walking out now," I replied, "and we're not going to sign your agreement with the association." We gathered up our papers and left him standing there, very upset with us to say the least.

Three and a half years of difficult struggles and negotiations had gone by and now we were back to "space A," having to start all over again. The local

media took up the cause and painted us as the
enemy of the city. For our part, we didn't know
what we were going to do, except wait and hope
something changed in either the neighborhood
association or at City Hall.

I do remember one final meeting with the
mayor, though. He told me that our best bet was
still to get out of town and build in the suburbs.
To which I replied, "Mister Mayor, with all due
respect, we'll see who gets out of town first." I
wasn't being disrespectful. I just knew God had
said we'd be a praise in the city, and I was
confident that, if the Lord wanted us in town, no
one would be able to run us out. Within two weeks
of that meeting, President Carter recruited the
mayor to be a member of his Cabinet. *He* got out
of town and did not return for years.

Shortly thereafter, I attended a pastors' prayer
meeting at the Portland Foursquare Church.
Without my asking, forty local pastors began to
intercede for our situation, waging fervent spiritual
warfare against any work of darkness that would
come against our church and keep us from
building.

I remember so clearly that whole group of
pastors praying for and laying hands on me, crying
out to God that He would release us to do His will.
As they prayed, I became aware that something had
happened in the heavenlies. Somehow I knew the
authority of the King had been released by our
brethren and that things would begin to change.
As I walked out of that prayer meeting I felt like a

load had been lifted off of my shoulders, knowing our long struggle was in God's hands and that He'd accomplish His will. Little did I know what that really meant or what was about to happen.

There were three main players in the neighborhood association, the agitators and spokespersons for the group. The first one lived next door to David Blomgren, one of our elders at that time. He'd gone to the University of Berkeley, was an admitted communist and atheist and hated Bible Temple. During the negotiations his wife had become violently ill, and shortly after the mayor's failed negotiations with us, she lay on her deathbed. She had her husband brought to her bedside and asked him to promise that he wouldn't fight Bible Temple anymore. She then, went a step further and asked him to actually help us get our permits. He agreed and that night she died.

I became aware that something had happened in the heavenlies. Somehow I knew the authority of the King had been released by our brethren and that things would begin to change.

The next morning, Sunday morning, the husband knocked on David Blomgren's door with his face as white as a sheet, explaining that his wife had died and that he'd made a deathbed promise. True to his word, he never fought us again and, in fact, did help us to get our permits.

The second leader of the neighborhood association, a single lady who lived adjacent to our property, also hated the church, and was very vocal in stirring up the neighborhood against us. Several weeks after our final meeting with the mayor, though, she died - in the middle of the night, without any prior sickness. We had been praying for her conversion, but she seemed to have pushed the situation beyond an acceptable limit.

With this lady's death the fear of God came into the neighborhood. Two of the most vocal opponents were dead. Disaster then struck a third lady, the head of the neighborhood association herself. She was in her mid-thirties and was truly a hateful woman. In fact, during one of the hearings, she actually got so angry she stabbed an elderly lady in the back with a ballpoint pen - in retaliation for the woman's simply having testified on our behalf. Within weeks of our final meetings with the association, though, she developed arthritis of the spine and was forced to walk badly bent over - unable to straighten herself up anymore.

> *God had said, "Enough!" - sovereignly bringing an end to the association's opposition. The power of the kingdom of darkness had been broken in prayer and the battle was quickly won.*

I didn't rejoice in these events. But evidently, God had said, "Enough!" - sovereignly bringing an end to the association's opposition. The power of the kingdom of darkness had been broken in prayer and the battle was quickly won.

Shortly afterward, the Lord gave me a plan. The Lord opened my eyes to realize that if we could just get some additional parking in the area we would be able to build on the commercially zoned part of our property. We had been proposing an addition to the old sanctuary but that was not zoned for commercial use. However, the old garage door company that we were using for our Christian school was zoned C-2.

I went down to the planning commission for another meeting with the chairman. For three and a half years we'd been in and out of that department. Normally, the chairman would meet me with a disgusted look on his face, but this time, the entire atmosphere had changed. I doubt if they'd heard about what had happened to the leaders of the neighborhood association, but as I said, I believe when those area pastors prayed, something broke in the heavenlies. This time, the chairman was warm and friendly.

To make a long story short, after that meeting the changes we suggested - changes to give us more parking and ultimately the ability to construct our new auditorium - were approved both by the planning commission and the neighborhood association without further hearings.

As with all growing churches, there came a time of fund raising. In the beginning, we just couldn't seem to get it off the ground. It was estimated that it would cost eight hundred thousand dollars to build the auditorium where we wanted it next to the old theater. That was a lot of money in those days, and no matter what we did, we weren't able to raise the funds.

Then, in the fall of 1976, John Gimenez, a beautiful brother from Virginia Beach, came to us. The Lord used him in an unusual way to get the church moving. I remember so well the night he spoke. He preached on giving to the work of God and challenged the people to rise to the occassion, challenging every family to give three thousand dollars - "one for the Father, one for the Son, and one for the Holy Ghost!" It was probably the most hilarious night of giving I ever experienced. The people came down the aisles with their pledges of three thousand per family, dancing and leaping with great liberty and joy. Before it was over, the entire eight hundred thousand was committed.

> *Though it took us seven years to see the work of the Lord fulfilled, the Lord showed himself strong; the will of the Lord was done, and God received great glory.*

I can't really communicate how excited the congregation was. We had acquired all the property needed, thanks to supernatural intervention. We had all the money pledged, and we were ready to build.

We began on a pay-as-you-go basis, and in the fall of 1979, we dedicated our new auditorium, debt free - what a marvelous demonstration of the grace of God! Though it took us seven years to see the work of the Lord fulfilled, the Lord showed himself strong; the will of the Lord was done, and God received great glory.

I've often referred to that time as the "seven year tribulation." When we finally moved into our new facility after such a long struggle, we rejoiced greatly. Yet the whole time we were struggling and building, we knew that facility was not our final resting place. From the beginning, the Holy Spirit had spoken to us that we were to "build to sell." As a result, we purposely designed our building with multiple uses in mind. I wonder if you can understand how frustrating it was raising hundreds of thousands of dollars, fighting with city hall, waging war with the neighborhood and the heavenlies, all the while knowing that the proposed structure would not be one in which we'd stay for long.

Still, the Bible Temple people proved themselves to be people of faith, a people who knew how to "follow the cloud," how to obey the word of the Lord no matter what the consequences, and even if it didn't always seem to make perfect sense.

For me, the seven year struggle had been overwhelming, and I arrived at the end emotionally drained. For the next two years it was all downhill. I entered into a wilderness experience - a period of burnout - the like of which I never experienced before and never care to experience again.

I didn't know what was happening to me, just that suddenly I didn't care about anything. It was so strange to have spent a lifetime in ministry and suddenly to have no heart for it - no heart for God - no heart for the church or anything else. I was like a boxer knocked out but still on my feet just barely going through the motions. Somehow I'd preach my sermons but then would retreat immediately to my little office where I'd sit alone in darkness, not bothering to turn on the lights. I didn't want to see or talk to anyone. I just wanted to do my job as quickly as possible and

> *I needed just to stay steady, stick to principles and pray.*

get out. This went on month after month for two years. I wondered if I'd ever be normal again.

I didn't know what was going on, just that there was no fulfillment and I'd lost my way. In retrospect, I wish there would have been someone there to talk to me - to explain that what I was going through was really not that unusual - that it was only for a season and that I needed just to stay steady, stick to principles and pray. That God was still with me and would never forsake me; and that if I'd continue to seek Him, I'd be like a pilot flying out from a dark cloud into the light. At the time there was no one around me who'd experienced such a thing or, if there was, I wasn't listening to them.

I struggled under this stange burden for two long years. But one Sunday, as I started up to the pulpit, I had this sudden awareness that I loved the people; I was excited about the ministry; and the fire was back. I had done nothing different and no significant event had occured. I had simply weathered the storm and flown out of the clouds with a renewed sense of vision and passion for the things of God.

To this day I don't know exactly what it was that struck me - perhaps it was the "let down" of victory after seven years of warfare and struggle. Maybe my adrenalin just quit pumping. Maybe it was a change of life. Or maybe it was something else. I just don't know.

While I'm not proud of the "auto pilot" nature of my ministry during that period, I think it was better to have stayed, going through the motions, than to have run away. The whole experience gave me new insight into how someone can throw away their career at the absolute pinnacle of their success. Since that time I've known other men of God who've gone on sabbaticals during similar circumstances and some of them have never come back. The enemy can use that vulnerable time to draw men off into more lucrative financial opportunities or a host of other temptations from which it becomes difficult to return.

In light of this experience, it is with great compassion that I offer this advice to anyone who finds himself in a similar situation. Stick to the basics, stay the course, and walk by faith not emotion.

CHAPTER 14

L ooking back on the consuming nature of our seven year struggle with the neighborhood association and city hall and the ensuing two year wilderness experience, I'm struck by how many great things God was simultaneously accomplishing in our midst. If I hadn't been so consumed with the building struggle perhaps I might have savored the other things even more.

❧

In 1975, my eldest daughter, Debra, was married to Phil Zedwick, a teacher in our Temple Christian School. I remember giving Debi away, teary eyed with the bitter-sweet feelings of any proud father, then immediately afterward, performing the marriage ceremony as I would later do with each of her three sisters. Debi's wedding ceremony took place in the old theater, while the others were married in the early eighties and in the new facility.

Debi's reception was held in a tent we had erected in the parking lot and five or six hundred people joined in the celebration.

As each of our girls grew up, we walked them with care through the husband selecting process. As a result, God placed into our lives four young men all committed to serving the Lord.

Phil graduated from PBC and in addition to teaching, has given much of his time and talent to encouraging both girls and boys in sports. Diane's husband, Mark Bryan, has beenan elder in Bible Temple for many years. Mark Sligar, Brenda's husband, led the publications department for ten years. He now serves as Bible Temple's business administrator. Todd Ebeling, Tracey's husband, has been one of the piano players for our worship services and for the choir. He and his father are in business together.

About my daughters, though, I've been asked if it got successively easier to give them away after Debi and my answer is an emphatic "No!" It got harder and the hardest was when Tracey, the youngest, left in 1984. That emptied the nest. However, instead of scaling down, others have continued to live with us and we wound up enlarging our family room. We rejoice today that our grandchildren have multiplied to thirteen, our latest born in July 1995.

In 1975, Edie and I had the opportunity to return to Ireland. It had been twenty-five years since Edie had been there - a country she most loved; and for me it had been fifteen. We took our daughters Diane and Tracey with us and had a wonderful family time with the always warm and loving Irish people.

But beyond that it was an opportunity to go back and make amends for the mistake I'd made there in the early days and to lay the foundation for some works that lay ahead.

I always think of Ireland in terms of the word *if* - if only I'd known in the beginning what I learned later on. In the early days, mine was like a Philip ministry, as we turned cities upside down with mighty miracles and healings;

> *I was handicapped with a blindness to the important role of local churches in keeping them saved.*

but unlike Philip we didn't call in John and Peter to follow up and set churches in order. In fact, as I've mentioned elsewhere, I didn't call in anybody, believing that evangelism - *getting them saved* - was everything; I was handicapped with a blindness to the important role of local churches in *keeping them saved.*

Thus, as I've also mentioned, I had virtually hundreds of young men following me - young men who, if I'd trained them - could have been raised up as pastors and the harvest wouldn't have been lost.

Edie and I and the girls went to Belfast and I ran an ad in the Belfast paper - a huge daily paper that reaches most of Ireland.

In the ad I identified myself as K.R. Iverson, not

knowing how many would remember me from the 1950's, and requested church leaders meet with us at a set time in the Belfast Hotel. I was gratified when about one hundred pastors attended and gladly took the opportunity to humble myself before them.

I apologized for ignoring them in the 1950's, explaining how I hadn't understood the need for local churches then - how I'd thought, as an evangelist, I was God's gift to their country. Then I

I hadn't understood the need for local churches

explained that I wasn't there now to build my name or ministry but would be pleased to help them in establishing their churches and in building up the kingdom of God.

In that meeting - in that prophetic moment - doors were opened and connections made that have important implications to this day. Now we have and/or sponsor various works in Ireland with more planned for the future.

Earlier, in 1973, a missionary Brother Leo Kaylor invited me to Japan. Leo had such a heart for the Japanese people and wanted for them what God was doing in Bible Temple.

In Japan at that time, there were very scattered, very tiny churches averaging around fifteen people to a congregation. A very large church totalled perhaps fifty people. In a sea of humanity - some one hundred million people living on those small islands - it wasn't difficult to understand why Christians felt overwhelmed and why the major emphasis was on salvation. There were just so many people to get saved!

An all Japanese Pentecostal Ministers' Conference had been meeting annually in Osaka and Leo wanted me to address the members chiefly because, after that particular year, they were planning to disband. They had become dispirited, I believe, because of the extreme seriousness with which they approached their salvation message - ie. "so many souls, so little time to get them saved." They neglected to make time for the joy of the Lord and bring the saints to maturity.

Rather than speaking to them about salvation - about some new or better formula for saving souls - I chose to tell them about the power available to them through their local churches and the importance of the local church. And it was a message that went over like a lead balloon with them. In fact, after a couple of days, Leo came to me and stated what to me was already obvious - the pastors assembled there just weren't buying it.

I offered to change - to preach on something else - but, after a minute of considering, Leo said no, to just keep on with what I was doing because, if they didn't accept it, they would disband anyway.

In the next meeting I continued, doing my best to outline for them what the house of God was supposed to look like. I compared David's and Moses' Tabernacles - the praise and worship and joy and singing and dancing that God was restoring versus the law which He was not restoring.

Suddenly my translator, Brother Nishihara

understood, however, and became absolutely transformed and energized. His voice went up about an octave and he began preaching to them speaking very rapidly and apparently oblivious to me for a good five minutes.

Finally, he stopped and turned to me. He bowed asking my forgiveness. At that moment the Spirit fell on the whole place. Voices were raised up for the first time in true worship as praises ascended in volume to the heavenlies.

As it turned out, it was actually a prophetic moment in the life of that nation and the Lord blessed me to be there as a participant. Instead of disbanding, the all Japanese Conference

> *At that moment the Spirit fell on the whole place.*

increased remarkably, so that today there are some five or six hundred members. Now there are churches all over Japan, some with congregations of up to six hundred or more people. As a result, many of the students in Portland Bible College are from Japan - more prospective pastors for the future.

Another prophetic moment in the development of our overseas ministries took place right in my office. A young Chinese-Indonesian man who was at the Bible college worked as a janitor at the church and would come into my office everyday to vacuum. His name was Jimmy Oentoro. One day, when I happened to have a little free time, I invited him to sit and talk.

I asked him about his plans after finishing

school and was interested to learn that prior to coming to PBC he'd started several campus churches in his native Indonesia.

"Pastor Iverson," he said, "I just didn't have the training to take them anywhere after I got them started. So, I decided to take time to get the training."

I liked him immediately and asked if there was anything we could do for him once he graduated. He said, he didn't want or even need money, but that he would like more than anything for us to ordain him and send him out as a Bible Temple minister.

We checked into his background some more and found he was, as he'd said, still plugged into the five or six churches he'd founded. The eldership met, prayed and decided to send him out as an ordained minister from Bible Temple.

That was a number of years ago and since that time the Lord has used him in great ways. In Los Angeles he started an all Indonesian church which rapidly grew to several hundred members. He then moved to Jakarta where he has esstablished a church of over seven hundred and growing. In addition, he's gotten involved in the networking of churches in that part of the world with one as far off as Tokyo. As it turned out, his family was very weathy and he'd worked while he was at Bible Temple, not because he had to, but because he didn't want to have it easier than anyone else. Because of his family ties, he's been able to touch the very rich in the Far East with the gospel of Jesus Christ. He has become a major player in that part of the world and conducts a ministers conference with nearly two thousand in attendance.

Today, pastors from our outreach churches in Indonesia, Japan, Ireland, England, and many other countries are members of our Ministers' Fellowship International (MFI) which serves more than three hundred pastors from all over the world. Many of those sprang from our own loins to plant outreach churches while the remaining have other origins but have come to identify with us.

Of course, as I mentioned before, it was not always like this. In the early days, when I first took over from my dad as senior pastor, we were ostracized by the main pentecostal churches in Portland. We were excluded because they said we were "latter rain." At that point, we had fellowship with only five small, independent pentecostal churches. The interesting thing was that, when we finally did adopt the principle of prolonged praise from the "latter rain" movement - the principle that brought our visitation in 1965 - the five little churches also left us.

Four shunned us immediately. When the pastor of the fifth called me to say he was canceling a joint youth rally we had scheduled, I asked him if he could come by my office and tell me why.

Of course, it was uncomfortable as he sat across from me sheepishly, unwilling to look me in the eye. I told him I prized honesty and asked him to please tell me straight. He took a deep breath and blurted out, "I'm sorry, it's that prolonged praise you're doing. It just makes me sick to my stomach."

Well, if he'd asked me to change almost anything else - cut my hair, grow a beard, whatever - I would have considered it; but he was, as I say, striking at the very heart of what the Lord had shown us.

I stood up and shook his hand saying I'd pray for him. Then a scripture leapt into my mind having to do with Joseph, and I told him, "Someday when you are hungry you can come back for bread."

Apparently, he took offense at that and avoided speaking to me for seven years. Then a strange thing happened. By that time our church was in the midst of phenomenal increase and I had just come back from a trip to Brazil. There, unexpectedly, I'd encountered people who already recognized me because of our tape ministry having gone before me. As I headed to our Thursday night service directly from the airport, I decided to speak on "fruit we don't know we have." Of course, the congregation was happy to have me back and after a joyful time of "prolonged praise," I began my message with the same scripture which had come to me in speaking to my fellow pastor seven years before - *"Joseph is a fruitful vine, a fruitful vine near a spring, whose branches climb over a wall"* Genesis 49:22.

As I looked out on the congregation, I couldn't believe what I saw. There was that same pastor sitting way in the back. The next day he came to my office and said, "I was hungry and you had bread."

As time went on, we became hosts of the

Northwest Ministers Conference meetings ministering up to eight hundred leaders. In addition, we started our own Fellowship of Outreach Churches, which in the beginning included just those pastors who'd been sent out from Bible Temple. Ultimately the fellowship was approached by other ministers wanting our covering and training. While at first our pastors resisted the idea, preferring the intimacy and, I suppose the "purity" of our own group, I eventually prevailed upon them to open the doors at least to those pastors who they themselves recommended. I did this because of two heart-wrenching experiences. In one month two pastors who called me -reaching out for help - fell morally soon after I'd been forced (by our guidelines) to reject their appeal. This lit a fire in me and, after my presentation at the Outreach Church meeting in 1985, everyone agreed that the time had come to enlarge our fellowship. Thus Ministers Fellowship International (MFI) was born.

Now we see everyone twice a year, at regional conferences and at an annual conference. There are, of course, informal visits as circumstances warrant. The principles God instilled in us in the mid-sixties have stayed with us, and it is those dynamics that have kept us and enabled us to grow even in difficult times. These principles are what we endeavor to share with the church leaders in MFI and ultimately with those leaders with whom they come into contact.

One of the greatest blessings has been the opportunity to enter into fellowship with leaders in the Portland area. Not only have we been able to fellowship with our pentecostal brethren (as seen in their wonderful support for us in 1976 when they prayed us through the trouble with the neighborhood association) we now have excellent relationship with our evangelical brethren as well. We now fellowship together in regular pastor's prayer meetings and occasional praise gatherings in the downtown Coliseum.

In 1981, the Lord spoke to my wife, Edie, that He was going to do something unusual in our "year of jubilee." It was Edie's fiftieth birthday - a milestone I'd passed several months earlier. We would both be fifty together for three months. Seated on the platform, Edie had just been presented with a basket of flowers by the ladies in the church when the Lord touched her heart prophetically.

❧

Edie was very excited by the touch, and very sure, she confided to the church, that somehow they would be included in whatever the Lord was going to do. However, that was all she was given at the time. We would all just have to wait.

The church continued to grow and prosper when one day, as I was working in my office, a retired air traffic control officer named Jack

Melligan came in to ask if there was some way he could serve in the church. Initially I just wanted to help him find something to do and, more or less on a whim, asked that he investigate the old Judson Baptist College campus and find out what was happening with it. Someone had mentioned they thought it was up for sale, and I remembered inquiring about it previously without positive feed back. In fact, they were so anti-charismatic there that they wouldn't even talk to me.

Not too long afterwards, Jack Melligan returned, saying the present owners were interested in talking. As it turned out, the college had already sold the campus to a group of developers. The developers, in turn, had received approval to build 600 condominiums on the "prime view" property located on Rocky Butte, a steep hill in Northeast Portland.

However, as the prime interest rate had spiraled up to over twenty percent in 1981, the investors found themselves unable to follow through with their plans. In fact, the high interest rates were strangling them and they were only too happy to talk to us.

We inquired into the amount they wanted for the property - two and a half million dollars - the amount the investors originally had paid. Of course, we didn't have two and a half million dollars. We'd just spent one and a third million in a seven year building project. Fortunately, we were free and clear financially. We had no desire to go into debt and frankly, we were still recovering from the previous ordeal. Worst of all, the United States was experiencing the worst recession since the Great Depression. It just seemed impossible to even consider this property. Before we gave a definite "No," however, we at least wanted to look at the facilities. They were terribly run down; the grounds had not been properly maintained for years, and the grass was two feet high. The development company was planning to demolish the buildings to build condominiums in their place. There were dorms, a kitchen, chapel, gymnasium, and some other buildings. To replace them would have cost around five million dollars. However, after careful study, we determined that the buildings were salvageable.

Still there was the seemingly insurmountable problem of raising two and a half million dollars during a terrible recession. In addition, it would cost one million dollars just to repair the property enough for it to be usable for the Bible College and the high school, not counting any future uses. It just seemed too much.

One of the things that made the property attractive to us, though, was the fact that it was in the city - which is where we were committed to stay. We studied the property further and found it to include thirty-three acres in all, located at the crossroads of two major freeways and a mere fifteen minutes from any part of the metropolitan area.

I sought the counsel of the elders, and we walked over the length and breadth of the property. With the pros and cons before us, we began to seek God for guidance and direction. We knew we needed a definite word even to begin such a project.

During that period I remember driving south on Interstate 205 freeway, heading straight toward Rocky Butte. I had been out speaking at a church in Vancouver, Washington, and was driving home by myself when suddenly the Spirit of the Lord came upon me with strong intercessory

> *I pleaded with God, "Give me this mountain, Lord! Give me this mountain!"*

prayer. I began interceding with great anguish of soul and with tears streaming down my face I found myself speaking prophetically to the mountain. Finally with a shout I pleaded with God, "Give me this mountain, Lord! Give me this mountain!"

It was as if I'd turned into another man, weeping and driving and shouting at the mountain. I was glad no one was around to hear it. They would have thought I'd lost my mind. Something had come over me which was beyond me. The spirit of faith had spoken out of my mouth, and I had pleaded and begged God to give me that mountain.

I believe that something happened in the heavenlies as a result of my experience in that car. From that time forward, with the elders' approval, we began to negotiate with the owners of the property. Over a period of several months, we were able to work out an agreement.

Then the people rose up and gave, once again, in a sacrificial, marvelous way. No, we weren't able to raise the entire amount required for the purchase, but we raised about six hundred and fifty thousand of it, plus the money needed to prepare the facilities for use. We assumed the outstanding loan of $1.6 million - as in the Lord's perfect timing interest rates had started down and the mortgage had an adjustable rate.

I remember over four hundred people crawling like ants all over the side of those thirty-three acres, cutting down grass and cleaning up the place. It was a beautiful sight to watch hundreds of people laboring with their hands, cleaning and painting and getting ready for the new Portland Bible College fall semester.

> *There was great unity and a determination to rise up and take the land for the Lord Jesus Christ.*

It was like looking at the walls of Jerusalem through Nehemiah's eyes, seeing them in ruins, yet knowing that everybody was with us. There was great unity and a determination to rise up and take the land for the Lord Jesus Christ.

When we learned the history of the campus on Rocky Butte, our occupation seemed even more meaningful. From the time that Europeans settled in Oregon, the hillside had always been the habitation of Christians. It started with a log cabin church. Then from 1930 to 1960 a Christian high school called Hill Military Academy was located on the land. In 1960 Judson Baptist College established itself and remained for twenty years.

Another interesting aside was the fact that Edie's father had been killed in a freak accident on Rocky Butte when Edie was fifteen, and it pleased her deeply that the Lord should bring us here. This was the "something unusual" God had promised her for our year of jubilee. It pleased her that we took the mountain that had taken her dad's life and proceeded to bring forth new life from it by proclaiming the gospel of the Lord Jesus Christ to the world.

During this time we had our 1981 Prophetic Assembly. During one of the services, Brother Ernest Gentile began to prophesy to the Bible Temple congregation: "I have planned to visit this people, saith the Lord. I plan to come above and beyond that which I have done up until this point. My presence, my presence shall come. My prophetic word will break out among the ministry. There will be people lying on the floors under the power of the Spirit. There will be people who will come and say, 'what is happening in this church?' And you will confess that God is visiting us again. For the Lord would say, I visit this place and I visit many other places that claim my visitation. But I come now, saith the Lord, to renew a work of my Spirit. I come to bring a new dimension of my power. I come to release the fountains of the deep. I come to release buried treasure within the hearts of my people. A glory, a glory will return. I would come, I would come in a new dimension. I would come, saith the Lord, and fill the program and fill the teaching to overflowing. But from time to time I will be pleased to be absolutely, sovereignly in control. And in those times the people shall fall as mown hay."

It appeared the Lord wanted to renew what He

had done when He visited us in 1965. We didn't know exactly what it all meant, but we were certainly open to whatever the Lord wanted to do among us.

After a summer of refurbishing and repairing we began the 1981 Fall semester of Portland Bible College on our new campus. We were all very excited! We called the campus the "Bible Temple Community Center," as ultimately - and in spite of certain pressure - I didn't want the church and the school to remain separated. The following year we were able to move our Temple Christian High School up to the new campus as well.

The 1980's were a very exciting time for Portland Bible College and Bible Temple. God continued to bless us mightily. The congregation continued to grow every year. People continued to go out from us and start new churches. Missionaries were sent out. New teams of leaders were being trained continually for every area of the church and school, and the purpose of God for the church was being fulfilled before our eyes.

By this time, in fact, we'd sent out dozens of church planting teams throughout the United States and many more overseas. We supported works in Brazil, Canada, Mexico, Japan, Indonesia, Malaysia, Australia, New Zealand, England, Ireland, and throughout Africa. Many of the churches we planted relating to other works in their particular areas began forming networks of churches which we then serviced through our book and tape ministries and through the organization of educational conferences.

The efforts of so many people stand out during that period that it would take most of another book just to mention their names, let alone their many feats of sacrifice and endurance. I apologize for not mentioning more of them here but would truly be remiss if I didn't pay personal tribute to two in particular. First I must mention Bill Scheidler. Bill was about to be ordained as a Lutheran minister when he chose to come to our Bible school to relearn the Bible our way. Upon graduating, he served in various departments of the church. He ministered by my side as Director of Pastoral Ministries and was always willing to help bear the yoke of pastoring the church. God has anointed him with administrative skills which he now uses as Dean of Students in Portland Bible College. Secondly, I must mention Roxy Kidder, my administrative secretary who also graduated from PBC. The Lord has blessed Roxy with verbal talents and with professional organizational skills that are simply incomparable. I am forever indebted to both Bill and Roxy for helping us to get through the complicated times of extreme growth and worldwide expansion.

While I was in Brazil ministering at a pastors' conference in 1985, I had an unusual experience with the Holy Spirit. I am not really a subjective person. In fact, I think I'm more practical by nature, but I've had times in my life when I knew God was speaking clearly to me. This was one of those times.

I was sitting there listening to my dear friend,

Raul Trujillo, preach in Portuguese. I was absently doodling on a pad of paper - not understanding the Portuguese - when suddenly I realized I'd sketched a perfect dome shaped building. I knew this absent doodle was a picture of the church the Lord eventually would have us build on Rocky Butte.

When I returned home, I went to one of our architects and showed him the dome I'd sketched out. I wanted ultimately for us to have a building that would seat three to five thousand people as well as accommodate our grade school and all the peripheral ministries of the church. I knew the Lord was giving me clear direction concerning moving everything up to Rocky Butte.

We discovered that the type of dome building I'd sketched did in fact exist. It was called"thin shell construction" - started from the outside with a canvas roof blown up by powerful generators and held in place until the outside insulation could be blown on. Next, the re-bar was tied together and a giant crane sprayed on wet cement to form the dome.

This dome building could actually be built for the same price as a conventional building, however, it would be very energy efficient which in our circumstance was an important consideration. Rocky Butte is located on the west end of the Columbia River Gorge and we get a lot of cold wind and rain as well as snow and ice blowing through in the winter. They told us we'd save up to fifty percent in heating and cooling with this type of construction. Ultimately that wasn't the deciding factor. I think rather it was God's unique design for this church, and it has certainly drawn the attention of everyone in the area, including thousands flying into the Portland airport.

At any rate, and to make a long story short, we gathered ourselves and launched out on another major journey which again would take seven years. This time the cost was nearly ten million dollars.

In 1986, before we began, the Lord had spoken to me, saying, "Son, it's time for Bible Temple to have a higher profile in this city." Up to that point, we'd spent very little money on advertising. Our growth had been largely due to friends bringing friends making this a truly unique word to me. At first, I didn't know for sure what to make of it.

However, on the day the outside of our domes were blown up (one having evolved to two) we suddenly became very visible to a good share of the community. Overnight people saw two huge domes inflated on the side of the mountain and wondered what they were. The newspaper got involved and before we knew it, we certainly had a higher profile. To this day, visiting dignitaries to Portland are brought up to the Bible Temple Community Center campus and shown one of the cities unique architectural designs. We believe God is going to use Bible Temple as a place of refuge in the city of Portland, and that is why He's given us such high visibility.

There was many a trial and tribulation to go through, however, between the beginning and the completion of the domes. There were seven years of faithful hearts and faithful giving. While I won't go into all the nitty-gritty details of the necessary fund raising here, I will say I've never known a people with as much faithfulness as our members. Our people have always responded to a true vision from the Lord and have always responded to the confirmed will of God. They are a people of prayer, worship, unity, and consecration. I have watched this spirit of unity move through them now for decades.

W e were about to enter into our greatest season of financial challenge. We still had a debt from the purchase of the property. However, we felt an urgency from the Lord that we should move on and build the domes on Rocky Butte.

ॐॐ

Before long the congregation had given nearly two million dollars to get the first phase under way. On top of that the people donated countless thousands of volunteer man hours. They had a mind to give and they had a mind to work. In fact, we became our own construction firm. We had up to thirty or more men employed daily in the process of building our house.

Yet with all the sacrificial giving and work, never once did we reduce our commitment to outreach in our city, the sending and support of missionaries and church planting. We were able to expand our own house without neglecting outreach and service outside our walls, and that was very important to me. I thank God that we did not get so caught up in the building of a physical structure that we forgot the true meaning and purpose of the House of God.

We were building the domes on a "pay-as-you-go" basis, and as we entered 1990, I realized it would take another five years to finish the project at the rate we were building. At the same time, the word of the Lord came to us concerning a harvest in the 1990's, so we obtained a three million dollar construction loan from the bank in order to finish the project quickly. By that time we had raised about four million dollars cash for the property and the domes, and we were committed to raising another one and a half million as soon as possible. We also had our old building on Glisan Street up for sale. With that sale the construction loan was to be enough to finish the project. That was the theory, anyway.

Then came one of the most trying moments of my life. We were going full steam ahead, finishing the project with the construction loan. As is usual, the bank was giving us a portion of the money at a time, paying for construction bills as they came in. Then, when we'd used about half of the loan money, the bank asked for a current estimate of the final cost of completing the sanctuary.

Well, it was a huge building project. The sanctuary was one hundred twenty thousand square feet, along with hundreds of parking spaces and landscaping. It was only natural that the bank would want an estimate of the remaining funds required to complete the project.

We began to calculate the specific costs remaining to complete the domes while the bank put a hold on remaining funds until we had all the figures. In the meantime, the construction bills continued to pour in until we had about four hundred thousand dollars worth sitting on the desk - creating a crisis situation.

I took a few days to get away to a hotel in an attempt to work on a new book. I had a vision to write a book laying out my understanding of the dynamics of the New Testament church. I wanted to write about my vision and hope for the restoration of the church in our day. I needed the time and space to meditate on the truth of God's Word concerning His House. It was there that I received the stunning news from Jack Louman, our church administrator, that we were going to have an eight hundred thousand dollar cost overrun. This was in addition to the four hundred thousand dollars in bills already on the desk. All told, this added up to $1.2 million that we would be required to pay before the bank would release the remaining funds from our construction loan.

Jack had met with the bankers and discovered that they'd closed our loan. Furthermore, he said they'd gone on to scold us for incompetence and said with disdain that they shouldn't have expected any better out of church people.

Well, I had faced a lot of giants in my life, but this one was too big for me. Sitting there alone in that motel room, it was like someone had turned off the lights. I had an experience of overwhelming darkness I'll never forget.

The demons of hell came into that room and began to laugh and shriek at me. I could literally hear their words. "Dynamics of the New Testament church. Hah! Some glorious church you're involved in. You'll be the laughing stock of the city when you go bankrupt. The message you've carried to the world will be mocked and scorned by all!" I could hear them scream in my ears and I literally fell to the floor, whimpering and whining like a beaten dog. This only made the screams louder. "Look at the man of God!" I heard the loud voices of doubt and fear, mockery and scorn, coming out of the mouth of hell. It was truly the darkest moment of my life.

What would I say to the people on Sunday morning? What would I say to our creditors? I could hear the voice of our critics. "I told you Bible Temple had overstepped themselves when they bought that property."

I must have laid in that position for an hour, feeling like I was dying. I had no strength or will to live. I kept saying to myself that I needed to get up and out of that room, but I felt too beaten to do so.

I'm not over-dramatizing that moment either. That's exactly how it happened. When I finally did drag myself to my feet, there were feelings of terror all around me. I found my way outside and, because the motel was at the edge of town and bordering a farming area, I began to walk through the fields.

I probably walked for two hours when suddenly I felt God beginning to breathe into me a renewed spirit of faith. I heard the still small voice of the Father say to me, "I will never leave you, son. I will not fail you. Finish all the work I've given you to do. I'll be with you. Don't be afraid."

Just a little while before I'd been on the floor of the motel room whimpering like a whipped pup, but now, in an instant, the Spirit of the Lord touched me. His presence surrounded me and filled my soul.

I had an experience I have never had before or since. I became so angry at Satan that I began to shout at him. I began to tell him what I thought of his diabolical lies. I hate to even admit it, but I was so angry at the devil I began to curse at him. I felt as though the wrath of God was bubbling up in my soul

> *"I will never leave you, son. I will not fail you. Finish all the work I've given you to do. I'll be with you. Don't be afraid."*

and while I'm not recommending this as a normal method, I'm simply confessing my experience at that moment.

I found that the more I walked the angrier I became at the devil, and the more confident I was that the Lord was in complete control of our situation. After several hours I returned to the motel room and asked God for a specific word. Then I opened my Bible and read one of my favorite scriptures.

> *"The Lord is my light and my salvation; whom shall I fear? The Lord is the strength of my life; of whom shall I be afraid? When the wicked,*

even mine enemies and my foes, came upon me to eat up my flesh, they stumbled and fell. Though an host should encamp against me, my heart shall not fear: though war should rise against me, in this will I be confident. One thing have I desired of the Lord, that will I seek after; that I may dwell in the house of the Lord all the days of my life, to behold the beauty of the Lord, and to inquire in his temple. For in the time of trouble he shall hide me in his pavilion: in the secret of his tabernacle shall he hide me; he shall set me up upon a rock. And now shall mine head be lifted up above mine enemies round about me: therefore will I offer in his tabernacle sacrifices of joy; I will sing, yea, I will sing praises unto the Lord. Hear, O Lord, when I cry with my voice: have mercy also upon me, and answer me. When thou saidst, Seek ye my face; my heart said unto thee, Thy face, Lord, will I seek. Hide not thy face far from me; put not thy servant away in anger: thou hast been my help; leave me not, neither forsake me, O God of my salvation. When my father and my mother forsake me, then the Lord will take me up. Teach me thy way, O Lord, and lead me in a plain path, because of mine enemies. Deliver me not over unto the will of mine enemies: for false witnesses are risen up against me, and such as breathe out cruelty. I had fainted, unless I had believed to see the goodness of the Lord in the land of the living. Wait on the Lord: be of good courage, and he shall strengthen thine heart: wait, I say, on the Lord. (Psalm 27).

That word gave me renewed strength, and I knew what I had to do. On Saturday night I called the elders of the church together and told them what had happened, what I had experienced, and what I now felt God wanted us to do. They sat there stunned, but they also heard the word of the Lord.

That night, with tears of repentance, we confessed our sins to the Lord. We confessed our lack of spiritual vigilance, unity, consistent persistent prayer and the fact that we'd taken the success of the Lord's will for granted. We got on our knees before the Lord and spent the rest of the night in fervent prayer and tears.

> *God stirred our hearts that night as the presence of God came into our meeting room in a powerful way.*

God stirred our hearts that night as the presence of God came into our meeting room in a powerful way. He told us He would stir the hearts of the people as well, and that ultimately we'd see a great victory.

Sunday morning I had to stand before the congregation, believing deep in my heart that God would stir them to rise up. The minimum we needed was five hundred thousand dollars cash, now, just to pay off the outstanding debts the bank refused to pay. Then if necessary we'd just shut the whole project down and wait. Yet we had a word from the Lord that we were to be in the domes in 1991. We knew it really wasn't God's will to shut the project down, but we also knew we had to raise half a million dollars in cash to avoid being forced into bankruptcy.

I had to make the same appeal in both Sunday morning services. I simply told them the truth just as I've written it here. I announced that we were going to have a prayer meeting that night to ask the Lord to give us five hundred thousand dollars.

The people were obviously stunned by the turn of events. They could have blamed the men who were in charge of the project but that was not their spirit. Instead, all that day a glorious spirit of faith came upon them and the atmosphere of prayer and expectation in the evening service was electric. That night, in fact, was one of the most miraculous services I've ever been in. I had no way of knowing how many would come. The devil kept harassing me all afternoon, saying there'd be only a small turn out and nothing miraculous would happen. I should have known better!

When I came into the service, the church auditorium was packed. We began to have a prayer meeting. We sang and worshiped the Lord and called upon Him with an absolute confidence, praying specifically that He would bring in the needed money.

> *A glorious spirit of faith came upon them and the atmosphere of prayer and expectation in the evening service was electric.*

While we were singing and worshiping, I asked

the people to simply come forward and give an offering as the Holy Spirit led them. To make a long story short, at the end of the service we had collected five hundred twenty-seven thousand dollars in cash. When I made the announcement at the end of the service, a great shout of triumph went up in that place that I'm sure caused the demons of hell to tremble. Satan had tried to destroy us and had been utterly and totally defeated.

The next day the word reached the bank that a miraculous offering had occurred. I made an appointment with our loan officer and the president and, though all the elders wanted to go with me to confront the bank officials, I just brought a few. When we went in for our appointment, the bankers had a very different attitude. In fact, they made every effort to be kind and polite, but I was angry. They'd blasphemed the house of the Lord with their attitude and with their words and had almost forced us into bankruptcy. I wanted them to know we weren't pleased!

> *Satan had tried to destroy us and had been utterly and totally defeated.*

At first the loan officer told us he'd just release enough of the funds to pay the immediate bills and then re-evaluate the situation. I responded that we wouldn't allow them to force us into another financial crisis. If they didn't release all the money immediately, we'd simply shut down the project and go back to a pay-as-you-go basis. Finally, we agreed to go into an early bond program to pay the bank off, and they released the rest of the construction funds.

After our miracle offering, God seemed to remove the financial pressure all at once. We were able to sell the building on Glisan Street to another church for $2.5 million and we ran a bond program to cover our indebtedness and pay off the construction loan.

The Lord had spoken to us that we were to be up on the mountain in 1991 to prepare for a harvest in the 1990's now our journey could be completed. The stage was now set for a historic moment in the life of Bible Temple.

The momentous occassion took place on a glorious Sunday in October of 1991. We had been at our Glisan Street location since 1959 when we purchased the old Granada Theater. Twenty years later we'd dedicated the new sanctuary on that site. Now we were going up to the mountain. We were moving our habitation to thirty-three acres where we could continue to expand into the future.

I'll never forget that Sunday; it was so alive. We'd gathered together for prayer in what was now our former sanctuary. We then formed a car parade and drove, with a police escort, to our new home. It was about a two mile drive between locations, and we formed a solid line of cars the entire way. In fact, when the first car arrived at the new property, some had not yet left the parking lot at the old building.

Several old classic cars led the parade. We put our orchestra on a large flatbed truck to lead what was really a very large worship march to Rocky Butte. What rejoicing filled our hearts! As we poured into the new sanctuary we found the same anointing resting upon us there that had been with us for the previous twenty-six years on Glisan Street.

Some had been concerned that the atmosphere of worship and prayer for which Bible Temple was known would be lessened by being in such a large auditorium. But I wasn't surprised when I saw the people rejoicing and praising the Lord in the new facility as if they'd always been there. We've always taught our people to focus on Jesus and not on their environment. I think we could worship just as well out under the pine trees.

> *What rejoicing filled our hearts! As we poured into the new sanctuary we found the same anointing resting upon us there that had been with us for the previous twenty-six years on Glisan Street.*

The Holy Spirit has certainly watched over this church and it has been something marvelous to behold. I have had some wisdom, but only by the grace of God. He is the All-Wise One who has guided us from the beginning. It takes my breath away when I think of His goodness to us. It is the Lord's doing, and it is marvelous in our eyes.

The dedication services in November were very moving, as we spent time reviewing the goodness of God. A video prepared for the event went back into the church's history and graphically showed us the miraculous dealings of God.

At times it seemed as though the Lord would miss the window of opportunity to intervene on our behalf. But God is not in a hurry. He insists on doing His work in His way. If we are constant and faithful, He will bring us along through prophetic moments step by step on our journey.

God is not in a hurry. He insists on doing His work in His way.

To see my life summarized on a thirty minute video was a profound experience. I wept as I saw again how good the Lord had been to me, to my family and to Bible Temple, and how He had blessed us in such marvelous ways. All the glory belongs to the Lord!

EPILOGUE

At the end of the building project I sensed the Lord telling me that he wanted to release me to go "over the wall" to His church worldwide. Thus I'd been seeking the Lord diligently concerning my successor as for a couple of years had felt pressure to do so. I believe it's very important to follow Biblical principles when changing church leadership and, though I had been praying about it, the Lord hadn't shown me either the person or the time.

౭౿⭒

In fact, all the Lord had shown me was the scripture that, "Joshua walked in the ways of Moses." Which led me to know my successor needed to be able to carry on the apostolic vision of Bible Temple and to build with continuity on the foundation that had been laid. Yet my successor also needed to have the gifts necessary to take Bible

Temple into the twenty-first century, to move on to a new level.

I wanted to make sure that I'd be involved in this transition while I was strong in mind and body. I didn't want it to happen while I was lying in a hospital bed needing to make an emergency decision. In his later years, Moses' strength was not abated nor were his eyes dim. When he selected Joshua he was at the pinnacle of his strength and I wanted the same thing to be true for me.

Edie and I had talked about who would take our place in carrying on this great work. We realized Bible Temple was not Dick Iverson's church, it was the Lord's. Therefore, we were determined to settle for nothing less than the Lord's choice to lead the church into the future.

I had so many wonderful leaders around me - any one of whom could have been my replacement. My son-in-law, Mark Bryan, was a strong consideration. Then there were men like Wendell Smith, Ken Malmin, and Bill Scheidler, who also could have taken the reins of the church. I knew I had to get the mind of God very clearly if the church was going to continue to grow along the path it had been placed on by the Lord.

Wendell and Gini Smith, who had been with me for twenty years, were like a true son and daughter to Edie and me. Wendel had an excellent gift and ability to gather people, and was a definite consideration. However, one day during my decision making time, Wendell came to me and shared his vision of planting a church in the Seattle area. God had given him some scriptures that seemed to confirm this direction and he spoke very confidently that this was the mind and will of God. Thus, since I was certainly not looking to hinder the will of God, we released him to go to Seattle.

After we made this decision, a strange thing happened. Suddenly the confusion concerning who should lead Bible Temple in the future left me, and I could see clearly who it should be.

The one person who kept coming to my mind was Frank Damazio. I'd walked with Frank for twenty years, the last twelve of which he had spent establishing a thriving work in Eugene, Oregon. I'd trained him in many ways as a young man but by now he had developed into a wonderful preacher and teacher and had proven himself as a senior pastor.

It seemed unlikely that Frank would be willing to consider moving back to Portland. Eugene Christian Fellowship was doing very well and certainly would not want to lose their senior pastor to Bible Temple. In addition, if he was willing to come back to Portland as my successor, I felt he would have to serve under me during a three year transition. That's a lot to ask a man who has his own work and has been so fruitful in the ministry. However, if it were the Lord's will to appoint Frank as my successor, I knew he would be willing to submit himself to the process.

I approached Frank and his wife Sharon and, as we met, I sensed an immediate positive response. As it turned out, they were both very open to moving back to Bible Temple. However, Frank and I each needed to go to our elderships to see if they also would bear witness. We needed unanimous consent.

There were more than 20 elders in Bible Temple and about twelve in Eugene. Both elderships were made up of very strong leaders, qualified men of integrity.

I remember my meeting with the Bible Temple elders as if it were yesterday. I sat among them knowing that some were hoping they themselves would be chosen as my successor. With some fear and trembling, I stated very simply that I thought Frank Damazio should be the next senior pastor of Bible Temple. You could feel a holy hush around the table as the leadership - some of whom had been with me for over twenty-five years - absorbed the idea.

One by one they began to express their love and appreciation for me, saying many kind things.

> *A prophetic spirit came into the room and a vision for the future of Bible Temple filled our hearts.*

They also said that, while I'd always be a father to them, for the sake of the future of the church they agreed that a successor needed to be appointed. Then they expressed agreement that Frank Damazio clearly was ordained to be my successor. A prophetic spirit came into the room and a vision for the future of Bible Temple filled our hearts. We knew it was right.

The report came that Eugene Christian Fellowship's elders had the same experience. There the elders had also agreed that Frank should be released to take over the reins of Bible Temple and that Gary Clark was to be his successor. It was an exciting day in both churches when it was announced that Frank and his family were returning to Portland, and in three years, would be the senior pastor of Bible Temple.

The quality and integrity that Frank Damazio has shown during our transition years has been outstanding. There have been times when we've differed on issues, but we've always been able to work these differences out smoothly without hurting the church. I highly respect Frank for that.

During this time, Pastor Frank has been very active in leadership and in ministry. The church has grown and prospered, and Frank's giftings and ideas have already greatly blessed us.

Even as I write, we are coming down to the final months of our transition. In October, 1995, I will hand the reins of this great church over to Frank, who, with the other elders, will lead us into the twenty-first century.

I plan to make Bible Temple my home for the rest of my life, though I'll be travelling frequently, ministering apostolically. Ministers Fellowship International now has over three hundred pastors, many who are my sons in the faith who have gone out from here all over the world. My last assignment will simply be to father them and to pastor other pastors.

For the last fifteen years I have felt the Lord calling me to this ministry. It is simply impossible to oversee a local church of three thousand and care for other pastors the Lord has brought into my life. Now I'll be able to focus on apostolic ministry.

As always, the future is in the hands of the Lord. Since the Fall of 1994, Bible Temple has been experiencing another mighty visitation of the Holy Spirit. It seems as though we are seeing Brother Gentile's 1981 prophecy fulfilled in a powerful way. We are still in the midst of this visitation so it's too early to say how it will affect us in the long run. It gives me hope that we are all being led into the third generation of this great church, and into the uncharted territory of the twenty-first century, by the cloud of the Lord's presence. We have always valued the presence of God more than anything else and are committed to staying in the middle of whatever God is doing.

As for Edie and I, we are very excited about the future and believe that God is ordering our footsteps. We thank God for the privilege of pastoring Bible Temple in Portland, Oregon all these years. We've been blessed in every area of our lives. Now our vision is over the wall, touching the lives of pastors and missionaries wherever the Lord might lead us, knowing that Bible Temple will continue to be strong and prosper until Jesus comes.

I earnestly hope that you've heard my heart as well as my words in this story. I have accomplished nothing on my own. It was the Lord who built the house. I was merely His vessel, aided from the beginning by the diligent labor of my family. I am so grateful to the Lord for each of my family members and look with anticipation to the future years we will share together.

Each stage in my journey has been truly fulfilling, and it's not over yet. It really never will be. Now we go onward to the next great adventure!

～∽

*L*ife is not just a series of minutes, hours, days and years flowing out before us in a straight line. Life is a series of interconnected prophetic moments - set times, mountain peaks along the journey - that form us and make us who we are.

～∽